I SOLD my MERCEDES at LOSS and got RICH

by

Sandeep V Dandekar

The Corporate Monk

BlueRose ONE

Stories Matter

New Delhi • London

BLUEROSE PUBLISHERS
India | U.K.

BlueRose ONE

For permissions requests or inquiries regarding this publication, please contact:

BLUEROSE PUBLISHERS
www.BlueRoseONE.com
info@bluerosepublishers.com
+91 8882 898 898
+4407342408967

ISBN: 978-93-7018-416-9

Cover Design: Aman Sharma
Typesetting: Pooja Sharma

First Edition: August 2025

Jeetendra Kapoor

Life is a script, my friend. Some of us spend our entire existence rehearsing the same lines, stuck in a comfortable loop. But every now and then, someone dares to rip apart the pages, walk out of the set, and step into the unknown. That's when a real story begins.

When I first heard about this book—I Sold My Mercedes at a Loss and Got Rich—I was intrigued. The title itself had a rebellious charm, a paradox that hinted at something deeper. Then I read the pages, and I knew—I had found a story that speaks to the heart, shakes the mind, and stirs the soul.

This book is not about selling a car. No, it's about selling an illusion. An illusion of comfort, of prestige, of a well-contained life behind tinted windows. The protagonist, a successful corporate executive, dares to leave behind the fortress of luxury and step into the heart of real India. The local trains of Mumbai, the street-side tea stalls of Delhi, the auto-rickshaws of Chennai—each becomes a stage where he meets life in its rawest, most authentic form.

I have spent over six decades in the film industry. I have played kings and paupers, villains and heroes. But let me tell you something—no matter how many roles I performed, no matter how much applause I received, the most unforgettable lessons of my life came not from scripts, but from the streets. From the chaiwala outside Filmistan Studios, whose laughter was richer than any bank balance. From the spot boy who, despite his struggles, had dreams brighter than the arc lights on set. From the rickshaw puller in Kolkata who told me, "Sahab, jo insaan jeena seekh gaya, woh hamesha ameer hi rahega." (Sir, one who learns how to truly live will always be rich.)

This book is a journey of discovery, not just for the man who embarks on it, but for every reader who dares to walk with him. It is a reminder that wealth is not always in the numbers printed in bank statements. Sometimes, it is in the stories we collect, the connections we make, the wisdom we absorb.

Krishna Bunglow, Plot No.26, Gulmohar Cross Road No.5, JVPD Scheme, Juhu , Mumbai - 400 049
Tel: +91 22 2625 6844 | 2625 6845 | Fax: 91 22 26240650

Jeetendra Kapoor

If you have ever felt trapped in a cycle of routine, if you have ever questioned the true meaning of success, if you have ever yearned to break free and see life from a different lens—then this book is for you. It will shake you, inspire you, and perhaps, make you reconsider what being 'rich' truly means.

So, fasten your seatbelt—or better yet, unbuckle it. Step out of the driver's seat and into the crowd. Let this journey change you.

Because sometimes, to gain everything, you must first let go.

JEETENDRA KAPOOR

Mumbai, 04TH APRIL 2025

Krishna Bunglow, Plot No.26, Gulmohar Cross Road No.5, JVPD Scheme, Juhu , Mumbai - 400 049
Tel: +91 22 2625 6844 | 2625 6845 | Fax: 91 22 26240650

Index

- Sleepless night reflecting on the boy's face and questioning personal values
- Decision to abandon luxury explained in detail (including specific planning of the experiment)
- Reactions from colleagues, friends, and family – specific dialogues capturing their disbelief
- First bus ride experience – sensory details of sounds, smells, discomfort, and human proximity
- Encounter with Kamal Singh (ex-defense personnel) at CST Station – his military bearing, transition struggles, and philosophical view on respect vs. invisibility
- The toy seller Parveen's story – single mother, survival tactics, limited opportunities, and dignity in struggle
- Chennai orphan Santosh's perspective – his optimistic outlook despite hardship
- Transformation after six months – specific changes in thought patterns, sensitivities, and worldview
- Closing reflection: No longer viewing life from behind glass, but swimming in it

Chapter 2: Mumbai Locals: The Pulse of the City

- Atmospheric description of Andheri Station during monsoon – humidity, golden light, vast human tide
- First chaotic boarding experience – pushed by the crowd, sensory overload
- Meeting Keshav the dabbawala – his appearance, efficiency, responsibility, and flawless system

- Exposition on the dabbawala network – Harvard-studied precision despite minimal technology
- Meera's story – a college student's daily six-hour commute, her study habits on the train, family background
- Her father's philosophy: "The money spent on tickets isn't for travel, it's for dreams."
- Ravi's heartbreak narrative – description of his lost expression, inter-caste love story,and family opposition
- The poignant moment of him stepping off without a destination
- Lata, the third-gender ticket collector – her struggle for dignity, societal prejudice, and quiet strength
- Sensory details of Mumbai local experience – the sweat, jostling, shared laughter, camaraderie
- Reflection on Mumbai locals as a microcosm of life – chaos, brutality, connection, and resilience
- Final scene of stepping off the train transformed from observer to participant

Chapter 3: Delhi's Streets: Chaos, Charm, and Conversations

- Vivid description of Delhi's duality – from narrow gullies to glass towers, from rickshaw pullers to luxury sedans
- The sensory immersion in Old Delhi – spice aromas, street vendors' calls, the tide of people

- Rickshaw journey with Iqbal – his physical appearance, expert navigation, poetic speech
- Iqbal's recitation of his verses about Delhi and their meaning – dreams sacrificed for survival
- Scene at India Gate tea stall – atmosphere, patrons, chance encounter with Colonel Rana
- The colonel's weathered appearance, military bearing, and profound statement about forgotten soldiers
- The emotional impact of his words: "People who fight wars never retire. They are just forgotten"
- Encounter with Sangeeta, the third-gender beggar in Connaught Place – their traditional approach, appearance
- Her painful story of rejection at age 12 and limited options for survival
- Her philosophical question about God making them different but society providing no place
- Extended reflection on Delhi's contradictions – dreamers and forgotten heroes, rejection and resilience
- Final scene capturing Delhi's sensory kaleidoscope – beauty and brutality coexisting

Chapter 4: Chennai: Of Autos, Temples, and Tea Stalls

- Sensory immersion in Chennai – heat on skin, roar of autos, aroma of filter coffee, sea breeze
- Wild auto ride with Arul – his driving style, personality, life philosophy

- Arul's dream of owning a tea shop – a detailed vision of what it would look like, taste like, feel like
- Scene at the roadside tea stall with Murugan "Anna" – his physical presence, method of pouring coffee
- Murugan's wisdom: "Life is like filter coffee. Some get thick decoction, some get watery coffee."
- Night scene near Marina Beach with watchman Ganesan – the lighting, atmosphere, and his lonely post
- Ganesan's migrant story – detailed flashbacks to his village, dreams of being a teacher, 40 years of displacement
- His poignant insight: "Here, they call me a villager. There, they call me a city man. I belong nowhere."
- Visit to Kapaleeshwarar Temple – sensory richness of colors, sounds, scents of incense and flowers.
- Lakshmi, the flower seller – her hands moving deftly despite the heat, her faith-centered perspective.
- Her unwavering certainty compared to corporate market volatility.
- Evening reflection walks through Chennai – the quality of silence, inner strength, temple chants in the breeze.
- Final insight: Chennai doesn't shout its struggles but carries them with quiet dignity.

Chapter 5: Bangalore: Startups, Struggles, and Shared Autos

- The atmosphere of Bangalore – technology hub contrasted with hidden struggles.
- Shared auto ride scene – cramped space, fellow passengers, overheard conversations
- Naveen's heated phone conversation – his appearance, manner, and entrepreneurial passion
- Dialogue about his startup journey – funding successes contrasted with family opposition
- His father's perspective: "Only rich people can afford to play with startups. Jobs are safe."
- The tension between security and passion, tradition and innovation
- Encounter with cab driver Shankar – his dignified appearance despite the circumstances
- His career shift from security guard to cab driver after the lockdown job loss
- His perspective on self-employment: "At least here, I'm my boss."
- Visit to "MBA Chaiwala" tea stall – unique signboard, atmosphere, customer interactions
- Karthik's surprising background as a mechanical engineer and corporate escapee
- His redefinition of MBA: "Mindset, Business, and Adjustment"
- Scene at co-working space with Rahul, the office boy – his quiet observation of startup conversations

- His journey of learning to invest while serving tea – transforming servitude into opportunity
- Final reflection on Bangalore as a place of reinvention – not promising success but offering second chances
- The essence of success: not where you start but how far you're willing to go

Chapter 6: The Bus Stops: Waiting for Life's Lessons

- Philosophical reflection on bus stops as forced pauses in rushed lives – contrasted with airports/train stations
- Majestic Bus Stand in Bangalore – vivid description of crowds, sounds, activity
- The young woman waiting with her phone – her appearance, the hesitation in her movements
- Her story of missed opportunity in Singapore – the weight of regret in her voice
- The metaphor of hesitating too long at life's bus stops until opportunities pass
- Transition to Chennai's T. Nagar bus stop – different atmosphere, different time of day
- The elderly man with his small bag – his crisp white clothing, calm demeanor amid chaos
- His farewell journey to his village after 50 years in the city – lost wife, children in America
- His profound acceptance: "Life is like a bus journey. You get on, enjoy the ride, and get off at your stop."

- Delhi bus stand near AIIMS – different atmosphere, different crowd
- Ravi, the single father with his daughter – their interaction, her entertainment while waiting
- His double-job struggle after losing his wife to cancer – the exhaustion and determination in his eyes
- Scene near Mumbai's Dadar Station – evening atmosphere, different tempo
- The young balloon seller – his dirty clothes, bright smile, luminous eyes
- His joy over a single chocolate despite living under a flyover
- Reflection on how gratitude isn't about what we have but how we see what we have
- Final thought on life's different waiting periods – waiting too long, leaving too soon, boarding wrong buses
- The insight that every journey teaches something, regardless of destination

Chapter 7: Street Food and Soul Food

- Reflective opening on street food as a cultural narrative, not just sustenance
- Scene at Churchgate station vada pav stall – crowds, movements, efficiency of vendor
- Prakash's surprising revelation as a Ph.D. in Chemistry – his speech pattern changing when discussing science

- His career collapse story – lab shutdown, hiring bias, transition to street vending
- His philosophy: "My respect hasn't diminished. Only my work has changed."
- Transition to Old Delhi's smoky kebab stall – sensory details of aroma, sounds, night atmosphere
- Gulzar's skilled movements over the charcoal grill – his hands telling a story of their own
- His former life as a wedding singer – the transition from microphone to skewer after DJs replaced live music
- His poetic perspective: "When people praise my kebabs, it feels like someone is applauding."
- Scene shift to Chennai's Marina Beach – different light, different crowd
- "Idli Amma" with her simple setup – the contrast between her age and energy
- Her 30-year commitment after her husband's death – choosing cooking over begging
- Her perspective on hunger as "the worst disease" – feeding paying customers and the hungry alike
- Her determination: "As long as my hands move, the idlis will be made."
- Final reflection on the hidden histories behind every street food stall – dreams, sacrifices, resilience
- The insight that street food isn't just about taste but about human stories of survival and dignity

Chapter 8: The Haircut Chronicles

- Philosophical opening on barbershops as social institutions – confession booths, debating stages, therapy offices
- Scene at Mumbai's Girgaon barbershop – rusty chairs, old radio, Hindi songs creating atmosphere
- Iqbal Bhai's character – age, steady hands, observant eyes, dignified manner
- His surprising revelation as a former poet – the conflict between art and survival
- His poetic recitation: "Tell the wind that I am still alive, Tell the clouds that I can still pour."
- Transition to Delhi's Paharganj roadside barbershop – different setting, makeshift structure
- The incongruous sight of a wealthy businessman crying in the chair – his expensive suit, watch
- The barber's gentle comfort and later explanation of the man's grief over losing his wife
- The insight that a barber's chair is where men let down their guards
- Scene shift to Chennai's T. Nagar – morning atmosphere, different clientele
- The nervous young man before his job interview – his posture, expression, clothing
- Murugan Anna's encouragement through both haircut and blessing
- The young man's return with news of success – the transformation in his bearing

- Kolkata scene with the homeless man – his longing gaze at the barbershop mirror
- The barber's kindness: "Every man wants to look good. Poverty doesn't mean losing one's dignity."
- Final reflection on barbershops as temples of transformation – not just changing looks but rediscovering self
- The insight that these are rare places of human pause and connection in a rushing world

Chapter 9: Tea Stalls: The Unofficial Town Squares

- Evocative opening on tea stalls as India's heartbeat – omnipresent across landscapes
- Midnight scene at Marine Drive – the darkness, sea sounds, flickering stall lights
- The midnight chaiwala's character – weathered face, kind eyes, nighttime wisdom
- The varied nocturnal customers – taxi drivers, night shift workers, the lost and lonely
- His insight: "Some people's nights are for sleep, but for others, it's an entire life."
- Transition to Old Delhi tea stall – different atmosphere, crowds, sounds
- The elderly man in the Nehru jacket – his isolation, distant gaze, lonely ritual
- His 20-year daily visit after losing family in an accident – the tea stall as lifeline
- The poignant realization that sometimes a simple tea stall saves lives by providing connection

- Scene shift to Chennai's T. Nagar – morning hustle, different clientele
- Young Rajesh in his crisp white shirt – the contrast with other tea vendors
- His engineering background and struggle to find employment – the shame turned to pride
- His entrepreneurial rebranding as "MBA Chai" – Marketing, Business, and Attitude
- Kolkata's Park Street tea stall – different setting, different crowd
- The group of women in sarees – their laughter, conversation, camaraderie
- The middle-aged woman's transformation from silence to voice – finding expression outside home
- Her revelation: "For the first time, I felt that my words mattered too."
- Final reflection on tea stalls as more than shops – as bridges between strangers, pauses in chaos
- The insight that sometimes the most powerful stories brew alongside the tea

Chapter 10: The Faces of Faith

- Contemplative opening on faith's many forms beyond religious institutions
- Hyderabad scene with Pandit Hari Prasad – temple setting, atmosphere of devotion
- The crisis of the Muslim family with their ill breadwinner – their desperation, helplessness

- The priest's extraordinary campaign for blood donations – initial resistance from the community.
- His powerful statement: "If we are devotees of God, then humanity is the greatest religion."
- The moving moment of recovery and gratitude – temple bells seeming to approve
- Transition to Varanasi ghats – morning mist, river sounds, spiritual atmosphere
- The man who had come to the ghats for 30 years – his posture, chanting, internal focus
- His surprising revelation: "I have no god"
- His journey from seeking external divinity to finding faith within – transformation through self-belief
- Lucknow's small Hanuman temple – different setting, unexpected scene
- The Muslim man in skullcap cleaning the temple floor – the apparent contradiction
- Rafiq Bhai's story of rebuilding the temple with his Hindu friend after communal riots
- His simple wisdom: "Humanity is the greatest religion"
- Vignettes of other faith encounters:
    - The wealthy real estate developer sweeping Chennai temple floors in gratitude
    - The beggar donating his one-rupee coin despite hunger

    - The atheist restoring a church out of gratitude for past help

- Final reflection on faith as action rather than belief – what your values make you do
- The insight that true faith manifests in kindness, not religious labels

Chapter 11: Conversations with Cab Drivers

- Reflective opening on cab rides as more than journeys – as stories waiting to be heard
- Rainy Mumbai evening scene – weather, traffic, mood setting
- Raghav's character – his age, speech pattern, calm driving style unlike typical cabbies
- His revelation of owning a textile export business – the rise and sudden fall
- The philosophic acceptance in his voice: "Life can change in a moment. You just shouldn't complain."
- Transition to Delhi cab scene – different traffic, different atmosphere
- The ex-soldier's disciplined presence – spotless car, crisp manner, military bearing
- His 18 years in extreme postings – Siachen, Kargil – facing death daily
- The struggle of military retirement – small pension, hiring bias against veterans
- His perspective: "Life should not stop at any turn."
- Chennai scene with Sundaram – the Tamil songs in his car creating atmosphere

- His proud discussion of daughter Meenakshi – her academic brilliance, dreams of studying abroad
- His extra four-hour shifts to fund her education despite knowing it will take her away from him
- The poignant realization of parental sacrifice: wanting children to fly away
- The widow cab driver in Bengaluru – her saree, dark glasses, firm hands on wheel
- Her transition from expected domestic work to pioneering as female driver
- Her powerful declaration: "Only those who give up feel fear."
- Kolkata's singing driver – his beautiful voice, the Bengali song's melancholy
- His abandoned music career to support family – dreams deferred but not extinguished
- Final insight that the person driving might have a story more extraordinary than your destination

Chapter 12: The Good, The Bad, and The Grey

- Philosophical opening on moral complexity – the absence of pure good or evil in human experience
- Jaipur vegetable stall scene – evening atmosphere, ordinary-seeming vendor
- The teacher's unusual demeanor – precise movements, refined speech pattern
- His double life: respected teacher by day, vegetable seller by night

- His daughter's medical school dreams driving his sacrifice
- Transition to Mumbai's red-light district – atmospheric description, harsh realities
- The sex worker using her earnings to fund shelters – her quiet activism despite circumstances
- The powerful contradiction: her own life in chains while breaking chains for others
- Kolkata tea stall encounter with the elderly orphan – his appearance, manner
- His creation of family for abandoned children despite never having family himself
- His simple explanation: "I was born alone. I don't want to die alone."
- Varanasi ghats scene with the young boy – his appearance, surroundings
- His story of the abusive alcoholic father – the violence, fear, suffering
- The surprising twist of him working to save his father's life – performing for money
- His profound statement: "He is a bad person, but he is still my father."
- Vignettes of other moral complexity:
    - The transgender woman finding purpose at a Chennai temple
    - The homeless man sharing his only meal in Hyderabad

- Final reflection on human complexity – not about perfection but choosing goodness in imperfection
- The insight that true character emerges in how we respond to our circumstances

Chapter 12.1: A Visit to the Kids' Cricket Coaching Academy

- Scene-setting in Dharamshala – Himalayan air, blue sky, pine scent creating atmosphere
- The chain of coincidences leading there – chai vendor conversation, hotel manager's suggestion
- The cricket ground discovery – the simple facilities, rugged field, practice nets
- The children's appearance – barefoot, oversized jerseys, makeshift gear contrasting with passionate eyes
- The sensory experience – leather hitting willow, running feet, focused gazes
- Coach Anil's introduction – his age, demeanor, watchful presence
- His 15-year commitment despite zero sponsorship or funding
- His philosophy: "If this passion helps even one kid fulfill his dream, that's my victory."
- Vignettes of the children's stories:
    - Rahul playing with a broken finger – his pain secondary to passion
    - Priya defying gender expectations – her perfect batting stance, determination

    - Karan walking 10km daily – his physical sacrifice for opportunity
- The cricket discussion during break – favorite players, inspirational stories
- The children's surprisingly sophisticated understanding of cricket legends:
    - Tendulkar and Gavaskar overcoming physical limitations
    - Kapil Dev's courage, Amarnath's fearlessness
    - Women cricketers proving their place in the sport
- Final reflection on the academy teaching more than cricket – teaching resilience and hope
- The certainty that one day, these unknown children will be discovered and celebrated

Chapter 13: The Weather Within

- Contemplative opening on weather as both external force and internal metaphor
- Mumbai monsoon experience – the drenching rain, flooding streets, commuter struggles
- Yusuf the newspaper vendor at Churchgate – his weatherproofing techniques, philosophy of adaptation
- The contrast between those who retreat from rain and those who dance in it
- The monsoon as romance for some, survival test for others

- Mumbai's refusal to stop – the dabbawalas, office workers, street vendors continuing despite weather
- Transition to Delhi winter scene – bone-chilling cold, fog, eerie atmosphere
- Babulal the peanut seller – his rough hands, visible breath, resilience philosophy
- His insight: "Poverty always feels like winter—it numbs you from the inside"
- The layers of Delhi winter – woolen shawls, historical narratives, emotional complexities
- Winter rituals – kebab aromas, Lohri bonfires, Republic Day celebrations in the fog
- Delhi's refusal to hibernate – the rickshaw pullers, chai vendors, street musicians continuing
- Chennai's relentless heat – the physical pressure, the bodily struggle
- Lakshmi the flower seller's deft fingers despite heat – her mental discipline
- Her wisdom: "The heat only troubles the body, not the mind"
- The forging effect of Chennai's climate – patience, discipline, endurance
- Bangalore's gentle climate – the exhale feeling, the misty mornings
- The young entrepreneurs in Indiranagar café – their relaxed creativity, different rhythm
- The insight that not every moment must be a struggle – sometimes pausing is progress

- Final reflection on weather as teacher – storms testing limits, winters creating solitude, heat challenging endurance, breezes reminding us to pause

Chapter 14: Lessons from the Journey

- Reflective opening on the transformation from experiment to awakening
- The stark contrast between isolated luxury and immersive experience
- First lesson on resilience from Mumbai – making opportunity from difficulty
- Meenal selling plastic phone covers in the rain – her entrepreneurial spirit, her game-like approach
- The rickshaw driver, chai vendor, and beggar adapting rather than surrendering
- Second lesson on kindness from Delhi's winter – warmth in coldest places
- The elderly man distributing blankets – his humble refusal of recognition
- Small acts of kindness – the free rickshaw ride, shared shawl, tea for a shivering boy
- Third lesson on endurance from Chennai's heat – choosing to be forged rather than burned
- Lakshmi's disciplined flower-making despite heat – her mental transcendence
- The vendors, auto drivers, and priests who worked through scorching conditions

- Fourth lesson on breathing from Bangalore – finding your own rhythm
- Kiran's decision to leave corporate life – the space to think, reflect, move at his pace
- The artists, techies, and retirees finding their tempo in the city's gentle climate
- Fifth lesson on journey as mirror – each location reflecting different aspects of self
- The train ride home – fields passing, reflective mood
- Final realization that the journey was inward as much as outward
- The insight that selling the Mercedes was never about transport but about transformation

Chapter 15: Riches Beyond Measure

- Contemplative opening on the true meaning of wealth discovered through the journey
- The contrast between the man who sat in the Mercedes and the man who now stands
- The shift from measuring wealth in currency to experiences, stories, and connections
- Being richer in understanding – the unspoken bonds in Mumbai's crowded trains
- The dignity of labor, endurance of spirit, beauty of everyday struggles observed firsthand.
- Being richer in empathy – the woman selling idlis at dawn in Chennai

- The redefinition of success – from corporate metrics to human resilience
- The father educating his daughter through tea sales, the auto driver's 14-hour smiles.
- Being richer in gratitude – seeing what was previously invisible.
- The taste of vada pav in Mumbai rain surpassing five-star meals
- The kindness of a stranger offering a bus seat meaning more than corporate courtesies
- The completion of one journey, beginning of another – the ongoing transformation
- Response to the common question: "Would you buy another Mercedes now?"
- The explanation that selling the car was a metaphor for breaking free from isolation.
- Final reflection on true wealth – not in possessions but in lived experiences.
- The insight that the richest person is not the one with most things but one who has lived most fully.

Contents

Author's Speak

No one could have predicted my eventual wealth when I decided to sell my Mercedes for a loss.

Naturally, I am not wealthy. My career, my bank account, and my material luxuries were all well-established by that point in my life. What society considers a "successful" existence was something I had worked hard to achieve over several decades, hopping from air-conditioned office to air-conditioned office, completing deals, and meeting targets.

Something had transpired, though, somewhere along the route. To be more precise, it seemed as though something had ceased to occur.

I had lost all sense of vitality.

Life in the Aquarium

To illustrate my point, I'll tell you a little-known fact: I've noticed that many successful people have aquariums in their homes.

Envision this: an ideal environment for a fish to live in is an aquarium. You can regulate the temperature of the water. The delivery of the food is punctual. It is safe from predators and bad weather thanks to the glass walls. There is no mess, no chaos, and no danger anywhere.

The enormousness of the ocean, however, remains a mystery to that fish. It is unaffected by the excitement of unfettered swimming or the draw of currents. Is it alive, even though it's alive?

That aquarium had become my existence.

In a shiny Mercedes, my chauffeur would show up at my house each morning. I would take my place in the rear, cocooned in the leather and shielded from prying eyes by the tinted glass. I was engrossed in my email scrolling through my phone while the streets of Mumbai blurred by me—visible yet intangible, here but far away.

From a gated enclave to an office building, and from an airport lounge to a hotel suite—my world had shrunk to a cozy cocoon. The same coworkers, the same chats, the same habits. Luxury hotels, business meetings, and gourmet restaurants were the same filter through which I perceived every city I visited.

I appreciate the luxuries I was able to earn, so please don't misinterpret me. However, when you let your comfort zone prevent you from living life to the fullest, it becomes a prison.

The Moment Everything Changed

An ordinary evening was the tipping moment. At a traffic signal, my driver came to a stop, and I, as usual, was engrossed in my phone. I was jolted out of my screen fixation by a rap on the window. A little boy, maybe around 10 years old, was outside selling garlands made of jasmine. He had tattered clothing and bare feet, but what he possessed in those eyes was an irreplaceable ray of vitality that I had long since lost.

Our gazes briefly locked. Within that brief encounter, I sensed a stirring within—a nagging concern that persisted in the days that ensued: Was I genuinely experiencing life, or was I just existing?

I slept poorly that night. The more I reflected on it, the more my worldview narrowed over the years. My horizons shrank in proportion to my rising stardom. I was only shown a selective fragment of reality, rather than the whole spectrum of human experience, including its ups and downs, triumphs and tragedies.

My decision to leave my aquarium and dive headfirst into the real world came quickly, but it seemed unavoidable.

The Decision That Made No Financial Sense

People thought I was getting a newer, fancier Mercedes when I said I was selling mine. They thought I was crazy when I told them I wasn't going to replace it and instead intended to stroll the streets of India's cities for six months while taking public transportation.

"Why would you deliberately choose discomfort when you can afford comfort?" a friend inquired.

My financial counselor advised me to patiently wait for a more favorable offer on the car, as she was worried about the potential loss I would incur from the sale.

However, a part of me was impatient. The need to wake up my senses and broaden my perspective on life, as well as to reestablish contact with the environment, was overwhelming. I thought the experience I would get would more than make up for the money I would lose on the car.

I started a trip that would alter my life in irrevocable ways, and I sold my Mercedes at a significant loss.

Six Months That Changed Everything

During the next six months, I explored other smaller cities while relying solely on public transportation, including Mumbai, Delhi, Chennai, and Bangalore. I endured squished shared automobiles, crowded local trains, and bumpy buses, and I walked kilometers through streets I had previously only seen through windows.

Not only did I forego fancy restaurants in favor of roadside stands and cheap accommodation but I also had the chance to converse with hundreds of strangers whose lives would never ordinarily intersect with mine.

In Mumbai, I encountered dabbawalas, who educated me on the importance of purpose and efficiency. I learned the value of perseverance from the rickshaw drivers I met in Delhi. I paid attention to the unfaltering faith of the flower vendors in Chennai. Startup founders in Bangalore taught me how to set my own standards for success.

These meetings were more than just chats; they were epiphanies. My numbingly comfy life jolted all my senses to life:

- Eating vada pav while standing in the monsoon rain of Mumbai
- The jumble of temple bells and traffic in the morning, in Chennai
- The sting of a winter chilly Delhi wind in an insufficient coat
- Observing a group of kids in a dusty area playing cricket using homemade bats
- Incense and jasmine waft from a modest shrine at the side of the road.

What matters most is that I rediscover the meaning of genuine human connection—not through scripted business meetings or emails, but through the spontaneous, unfiltered talks that occur when you sit next to someone on a packed bench or endure a delayed train.

Digital Isolation vs. Human Connection

One of the most startling realizations during my journey was understanding how our increasingly digital lives are cutting us off from real human connection.

Think about it: In my generation, when we left home, we observed the world around us. We noticed faces, expressions, troubles, and joys. We struck up conversations with strangers. We were present in that moment because there was nothing else to occupy our attention.

Today, the moment people step out of their homes, they plug earphones into their ears and eyes into their phones. They move through physical spaces without ever truly being present in them. The 360-degree awareness of life around them has been replaced by a narrow focus on a small screen.

This digital isolation only compounds the bubble that success and comfort create. We are more connected virtually than ever before yet increasingly disconnected from the physical world around us.

Why I Wrote This Book

I wrote this book for those who, after attaining conventional success, nevertheless feel that something is lacking. If you feel like you're looking through a glass window instead of leaving it, this is for you. For individuals who, like myself, have unknowingly constructed spheres of solace that have obstructed true interpersonal communication.

This in no way implies disapproval of monetary success or comfort. The call is for a more balanced approach, one that includes genuine participation in the whole range of human experience alongside these accomplishments.

"I Sold My Mercedes at a Loss and Got Rich" is more than just a clever title; it expresses the straightforward reality of what transpired. I acquired wealth that money couldn't buy by giving up wealth that was tangible.

What To Expect From This Book

Follow me as I take you on a tour of crowded train cars and serene temple courtyards, through drenched marketplaces and scorching streets, in the chapters that come next. More about life, perseverance, and happiness than I could have learned from any corporate conference came from meeting remarkable regular people.

In this book, you will find information regarding:

- Mumbai and its residents, where events happen at a dizzying pace and complete strangers become extended families for a little while.
- Delhi's streets, where modernity and history meet, and extraordinary ingenuity is frequently required for survival.
- Peaceful nooks of Chennai, where spirituality and tradition teach us to be patient and have a broad view.
- Bangalore's blend of technology and culture, where old and modern India discover ways to cohabitate.

The point of these stories is not to glorify hardship or portray poverty in a positive light. It is important not to downplay the seriousness of the problems that many Indians confront on a daily basis. On the contrary, these anecdotes shed light on the remarkable strength, wisdom, and dignity that are present in the face of adversity.

I wish for this book to be a reflection of life's facets that you may have missed and a conduit to other viewpoints and experiences that differ from your own.

Maybe it will motivate you to come up with your own "selling the Mercedes"—discovering actions, no matter how tiny, that push you out of your comfort zone and into direct interaction with the world.

Because nothing good ever comes out of being encased in glass. This is what occurs when we muster the courage to leave the safety of our little bubbles and dive headfirst into the wonderful, unpredictable, and overwhelming ocean of human experience.

True wealth is waiting for you there.

Chapter 1:
The Aquarium and the Sea

Life Behind Glass

My life used to feel like a never-ending loop of ease and control. My corporate position was a palace of privilege, with its frequent encounters with prominent people and expensive benefits. My chauffeur would arrive at my guarded home every morning in a shimmering Mercedes, encased in a cocoon of leather seats, tinted windows, and carefully orchestrated stillness. I was able to float through the mayhem of Indian streets, oblivious to everything going on around me, because it blocked out the world. But I couldn't get the feeling that something wasn't quite right: was this actually alive?

My day-to-day activities had grown mechanically predictable. Each morning at six o'clock, I would be roused by the soft sound of an alarm, and then, presented on delicate porcelain, a meticulously cooked breakfast. Ramesh, my driver, will be waiting outside the immaculately polished silver Mercedes at 7:30. As I found my place in the rear seat, the soft leather would envelop me, and the soothing sound of the air conditioner would envelop me in a tranquil bubble.

"Good morning, sir," Ramesh would say, glancing momentarily into the rearview mirror at me. Reports indicate that Linking Road is experiencing heavy congestion today. I'll opt for the detour.

Whenever someone nodded, I would dive headfirst into my phone, answering calls, reviewing presentations, and checking emails. With the tinted windows and the constant purr of a German engine separating me from the outer world, the world outside would become a kaleidoscope of colors and motions.

During my time at work, I would go from a climate-controlled vehicle to an elevator to a corner office with sweeping views of the city below. I had a jam-packed schedule full of meetings: management strategy sessions, calls with international clients, and fancy lunches at places where the wait staff knew my order without me even asking. My day would continue with another round of meetings, choices, and controlled interactions at the workplace until Ramesh reappeared in the evening, prepared to take me back to my residential enclave.

Immaculate, climate-controlled, and reliable—that was my aquarium. Even though I couldn't sense it, I could see the outer world. I was shielded from its ugliness, its mayhem, and its unpredictability—and, unwittingly, its warmth, its authenticity.

The Moment Everything Changed

On an ordinary evening on my way home, the moment of truth arrived. We normally speed by this signal without stopping, but the traffic was somewhat heavier than normal. While engrossed in an email, I peered out the tinted windows of the car and saw a little child selling flowers at the traffic light. He couldn't have been older than ten.

Sweat and filth covered his face, and his enormous, torn shirt added to the unattractiveness. He exuded an air of quiet dignity, in contrast to the other kids who would throng around expensive cars making scripted demands. Gradually, he made his way from car to automobile, presenting jasmine garlands with a small bow that was devoid of the desperate motions that had become commonplace.

He came up to our car and softly tapped on the window. As it is my habit after years of training, I would have ignored it. I was compelled to look up this time, though. For a split second, we locked gazes. His were unambiguous, vigilant, and shockingly vibrant—neither accusatory nor imploring. A simple strand of white flowers, which appeared more real than anything in my air-conditioned cocoon, was held up by him like a garland.

The light turned green just as I was about to lower the window, preventing me from reaching for my money. Ramesh, ever the efficient, drew away from the boy and left him behind. I had a last glimpse of him, unfazed, in the rearview mirror as he continued toward the next vehicle.

"Should I have stopped, sir?" Seeing that I was staring at myself in the reflection, Ramesh inquired.

My automatic response was, "No, it's fine." It was not good, though. My carefully maintained equilibrium had been thrown off by that fleeting connection.

A Sleepless Night of Reflection

I was unable to fall asleep that night. I was troubled by the boy's resolute countenance; his strength in the face of adversity stood in sharp contrast to my sheltered life. While I dozed off on my king-sized bed, adorned with Egyptian cotton sheets, old, long-buried questions started bubbling to the surface.

What was his name? How did he spend the nights? Has he attended classes? To what did he aspire? Why did he crack a smile? Was he doomed to spend his life on the outside, staring in, or had he ever hopped in a car similar to mine?

Afterwards, the focus shifted to the individual. In all my years of social and professional interactions, when was the last time I had a genuine connection with another human being? When was the last time I felt the life and blood of the city I called home, not from some distant vantage point like a corner office or a fancy vehicle, but right where it beats? How long had it been since I was moved by something genuine, unfiltered, and uncontrollable?

For a long time, I had no idea that I had been living in an artificial, albeit secure and comfortable, aquarium. My entire surroundings were constructed with the express purpose of keeping me safe from pain, from uncertainty, and from the ugliness of the actual world. I was ensnared by the barriers of luxury I had erected around myself.

The moment has come to venture out into the vast, uncharted, and very real ocean of life.

The Decision That Made No Sense to Everyone But Me

I convened a meeting of my senior staff the following morning. I told them I was going on a six-month sabbatical after we had gone over some standard business stuff.

Our COO Asha inquired, "Are you unwell?" with genuine worry in her voice.

"Absolutely not," I responded. "I'm taking time to... reconnect with reality."

Many people were perplexed or even scared when I told them I was planning to sell my automobile and rely only on public transportation.

I was questioned by Vikram, my CFO, on why someone would knowingly choose discomfort. "You've worked hard for these privileges."

"That's precisely the problem," I pointed out. These advantages are now standing in the way. The world has become hazy for me.

Many people, including those closest to me, were shocked and skeptical when I announced my intention to forego my pampered lifestyle in favor of public transportation.

"Are you crazy?" my brother asked me when we were on the phone. The car should be retained. How will we handle a crisis?"

"You'll come to regret this decision in a week," my executive neighbor warned me. "The novelty will wear off when you're standing in your first overcrowded train."

My mom, who is typically on board with my choices, was worried, too. "Beta, people have high expectations for someone in your position and age. What do you suppose they'll say?

Their responses, however, simply served to reinforce my own suspicions: that I had let myself get ensnared by external validation of my achievement and the hollowness it seemed to bring.

Rather than seeking solace, my intentions were to seek connection, comprehension, and a more profound feeling of direction. A lot of the time, you must let go of other people's expectations of what you should value in order to locate these things.

Planning the Escape from My Aquarium

I devised an idea to explore the busy cities of India—Mumbai, Delhi, Chennai, and Bangalore—exclusively on public transportation over the subsequent six months. The local trains, buses, cars, shared rides, and even the rare bike rickshaw would all become my new travel companions.

Instead of eating at restaurants, I would stop at street sellers for tea and eat street food. I would forget about the world beyond the tinted window of my automobile. Instead of viewing life through the eyes of a tourist, I would immerse myself in the experiences of my fellow citizens, striking up conversations with strangers and seeing sights I would never have seen otherwise.

The logistics were surprisingly complicated. I had to rearrange my work duties, get my house ready for an extended absence, and sell my car—much to my accountant's disappointment—at a big loss. I had to learn to live without the help of the people I'd become accustomed to, find out how to use public transportation, and pack for a bag instead of a suitcase.

The city I thought I knew well from seeing it mostly from a car window or a high-rise office window—Mumbai—was where I chose to begin my exploration. Spending about six weeks in each city, I would then travel to Delhi, Chennai, and Bangalore.

The night before I set out on my journey, I stood in my roomy living room, taking in all the artwork, designer furnishings, and views of the city lights that surrounded me as signs of my success. I had a fleeting moment of uncertainty. Was my behavior naive? Feeling a little wild? Would I come back in six months, completely bereft of knowledge other than a deeper gratitude for my advantages?

Recalling the youngster at the traffic light brought up a flood of memories—his serene dignity, the intensity of his eyes, and the fact that we were only separated by a vehicle window, despite the vast differences in our worlds. It was imperative that I cross that threshold, emerge from my terrarium and into the ocean.

The First Step

It was more difficult than I had anticipated to give Ramesh the key to my car that morning. For seven years, he drove me around and, in his own way, protected me from the outside world.

With a look of true concern on his face, he questioned, "Sir, are you sure about this? At least let me drop you at the bus stop."

As I pressed the keys into Ramesh's palm, I remarked, "I need to walk there myself. That's the whole point."

To make sure he wouldn't lose his job due to my personal experiment, I had him collaborate with another executive in the organization. He wished me well and nodded, as if he understood but did not agree.

I made my way to the closest bus stop while carrying a light bag that had only essentials including clothing, toiletries, a notebook, and few electronics compared to my usual gear. Even though I drive by it every day on my way home, I finally paid attention to the landmark that was only a kilometer away.

I looked around like a first-time tourist. People in all sorts of attire waited patiently in line: students with bags, women in vibrant sarees carrying tiffin boxes, and men in business clothes. Their expressions varied from eagerness and exhaustion to quiet determination.

There was a brief upsurge of activity when the bus finally pulled up, which was, as I would discover later, the norm, ten minutes late. People boarded with a deliberate, almost orchestrated flow, rather than the disorderly stampede I had anticipated.

I fought my way through the throng, unsure of the unspoken regulations that controlled this routine every day. In the end, I managed to cram myself into a seat between a mother who was rocking a napping toddler. As the bus chugged ahead, she moved around a bit to make room, and the child's head flopped against her shoulder.

My adventure commenced with it.

Initial Discomforts

The initial few days were a sensory overload that put my adaptability to the test. My car's air conditioning, regularity, and sense of control were all things I longed for.

Instant and inevitable were the bodily pains. My clothing became clingy in the matter of minutes as the climate control failed to ward off the scorching Mumbai heat. Constant honking of horns, merchants' cries, machinery, and innumerable discussions made it hard to think coherently. On one hand, you could smell delicious street food or incense wafting from nearby shrines, and on the other, you could smell open drains or exhaust fumes.

My patience and strongly established sense of personal space were put to the test by the overcrowded buses, the disorganized schedules (or lack thereof), and the continual closeness to strangers.

Despite this, I started to pay more attention to the details of my surroundings than before, all because I was so uncomfortable. In a climate-controlled vehicle, you can't hide behind your phone, so you have to pay attention, which is something I have grown to dislike.

Promptly assembling the spicy snack, the vendor stood outside the bus depot, selling hot vada pav. In a matter of seconds, with deftness that betrayed years of skill, he topped fresh pav with green chutney, added a fried potato patty, sprinkled garlic and chili powder on top, and wrapped it in newspaper.

At a stall, a young couple were bickering in a lighthearted manner over their morning tea, with laughter drowning out their arguments. Her mischievous eyes danced as she teased the man with something I couldn't hear as she tugged at his sleeve.

An old man sat in a corner of the bus, his expression one of deep absorption as he stared out the window, holding a tattered fabric bag. His wrinkled face conveyed tales I could only speculate about, and his worn hands bore witness to a life's labor about which I knew nothing.

I came to see that inside every individual was a story—a tale molded by hardships, aspirations, and an indomitable will to endure. All of it had been lost on me in my past existence.

Unexpected Connections

As I relaxed on a Mumbai local train one evening, a guy in his fifties started talking to me. Ram, a manufacturing worker, was making his way home after a long and exhausting shift. In spite of his calloused hands and grease-stained clothing, the warmth radiating from his gaze was contagious.

"Aap pehli baar local mein ho?" ~ "Is this your first experience riding a local train?" He inquired with a little smile.

As soon as I gave him the go-ahead, he began to describe his life in great detail. He recounted his journey from Uttar Pradesh as a migrant, the hardships of a chawl mother, and the joy he had for his oldest son, an engineer who had just graduated.

"Yeh train to bas ek saadhan hai, sahab. Zindagi ki kahani to yahaan hoti hai" ~ "This train is just a medium, sir. Life's real

story unfolds here," he continued, pointing to the packed compartment.

The train shook along the rails as we conversed, pausing at stations where some alighted and others crammed in. Ram filled me in on the history of communities I had only ever seen from a distance by pointing out notable sites seen through the windows.

He appeared surprised when I asked him if the daily travel, long hours in the factory, and constant effort to make ends meet ever got to him.

"Thakaan to hoti hai, lekin zindagi rukti nahi" ~ "Fatigue happens, but life doesn't stop," he said without hesitation. I was able to work at a factory since my dad pulled a handcart throughout his life. For the sake of my son's office job, I toil away in a factory. Passed down from one generation to the next, this is more than simply my narrative; it is our nation's story.

I couldn't shake his statements, even after the train ride ended. I learned a great lesson from his resilience and modesty: the best moments of life usually come from the most ordinary places, and the best way to judge success is not by our own accomplishments but by the chances we give to other people.

A Soldier's Struggle for Dignity

I met Kamal Singh, a security guard and former member of the defense forces, inside Mumbai's iconic CST Station. Straight back, square shoulders, and attentive eyes—that was his military bearing. During his twenty-two years of service, he was stationed in some of the most perilous border regions as an officer in the Indian Army.

While I was asking him for directions, we started talking. He had an educated mind; his directions were clear and concise; and when I told him I was traveling to learn more about India, he offered me to have tea with him at a nearby stand when he was on break.

We shared mugs of milky, sugary tea while he told me his tale.

The words "when I wore the uniform, people respected me" came out of his mouth with a trace of nostalgia. Serving my country gave me dignity, even though I wasn't wealthy or powerful. I went completely unnoticed the day I retired.

It was difficult for Kamal to secure a fulfilling job, even though he had an impeccable record of service. His pension was small, and many employers didn't want to hire him because of his advanced age of fifty. The job of a bank security guard, where he stood guard for twelve hours every day, eventually became his home.

"I can't help but notice the irony," he remarked, barely suppressing a grin. Our nation's frontiers were formerly defended by me. Right now, I'm watching over an ATM.

His philosophical perspective on respect vs. invisibility was what truly stood out to me, rather than his complaint (which was more of a statement of facts than a complaint in and of itself).

"In our society, we respect the uniform, the position, the wealth—not always the person," he pointed out. Everyone could see me in my uniform. I feel like I'm just another piece of furniture now that they ignore me. However, at my core, I am the same guy—still committed to my principles, having had the same education, and always ready to provide a hand.

After we finished our chai break, he went back to his station, and I saw him straighten up, be vigilant again, and carry on with his work as if he had been at the border. He was dignified not because he was famous or wealthy, but because he knew his own value and lived up to it.

A Mother's Fight for Survival

At a crowded intersection in a Delhi market, I encountered Parveen, a vendor selling toys on a makeshift mat. She sat silently, rearranging handcrafted dolls and tiny plastic toys, in contrast to the other vendors who shouted at passers-by.

I paused to examine her wares because of her composed expression. She informed me while I perused that her husband left her and their two children three years ago, and that she was now a single parent.

"Babuji, yeh khilone bechke din ka ₹200-300 milta hai. Bas itna ki ghar ka ration aa jaye." ~ "Excuse me, sir, but I purchase food for the family every day with the ₹200-300 that I get from selling these toys."

'Why didn't she get a more secure job?' I wanted to know. In a melancholy smile, she blinked.

"Kaun rakhega ek unpadh aurat ko? Main sirf ek hi cheez likhna janti hoon—apne bachon ke naam." ~ "Who will hire an uneducated woman? I only know how to write my children's names."

Regardless of these constraints, Parveen had devised methods to ensure his existence. Seasonal toy sales were her specialty. She had made arrangements with a wholesaler to purchase goods on credit and settle the bill upon sale. With the help of other women vendors, she had developed an informal alliance; they would take turns watching each other's items when one needed to go to the restroom or obtain lunch.

The thing that struck me the most was how hell-bent she was on keeping her kids in school. She proudly displayed a little notebook that meticulously documented every penny, prioritizing the payment of school tuition before everything else.

With her convictions crystal clear, she declared, *"Mere bachche padh likh kar naukri karenge, to unhe kabhi footpath pe nahi baithna padega."* ~ "My children will never have to sit on the pavement if they get educated and find jobs."

The impact of her remarks was devastating. Every day, this woman got out of bed, battled for her life, and never once grumbled. I couldn't help but think of all the times I'd passed women like her and ignored them, much like the constant noise of the city.

An Orphan's Optimism

Santosh was an orphan who worked at a roadside diner in Chennai; he was seventeen years old when we met. His contagious positivity brought customers to his counter, even though he had a troubled upbringing in an institution.

With a smile that extended to his eyes, he served morning commuters idlis and dosas with swift speed, remembering regular customers' preferences without being asked.

While the morning rush was dying down, I approached him and inquired how he was able to be so positive no matter what was going on.

"Log sochte hain ke bina maa-baap ke jeena dukh ki baat hai. Par sahib, main toh bas jeena chahta hoon. Jo hai, usme khush rehna seekh gaya hoon." ~ "People think living without parents is sad. But sir, I just want to live. I've learned to be happy with what I have."

Even though Santosh's dreams were modest, he shared them with me, nevertheless. Instead of staying at the restaurant, he planned to save up for a little room rental. He had aspirations of becoming a hotel employee after he had mastered the English language. In order to enjoy cricket matches, he yearned for a smartphone.

I was struck by his total absence of pitying himself. I could tell he was perplexed when I inquired whether he ever felt furious at the fate that had befallen him.

"Gussa karne se kya milega, sir? Zindagi wohi rahegi, bas mood kharab ho jayega." ~ "What will I get from anger, sir? Life will remain the same, only my mood will be spoiled."

His concept was straightforward but profound: although some people are always moaning about how they don't have enough, he taught us to be grateful for what we have. Not because I felt bad about it, but because I had a new appreciation for it, I questioned my own privilege at that time.

The Transformation

When the six months were up, I had changed drastically from the day I got out of that Mercedes. Now that I felt truly connected to the world, the corporate aquarium I had once lived in seemed like a distant past.

Both the histories of other people and my own long-lost parts have been uncovered. I felt a more profound sense of empathy, not only the intellectual sort that recognizes the difficulties other people face from a distance, but the more physical kind that develops from having been through something similar. I had seen resilience in action and started to foster it in myself; it had evolved from a leadership seminar buzzword into something more tangible. An attitude of gratitude had taken hold of me, and it was not limited to material possessions; it extended to the relationships I had formed, the wisdom I had gained, and the splendor I had overlooked before.

Things had changed in my thinking. I now see individuals overcoming obstacles by using their imagination and willpower, rather than issues or inefficiencies that need fixing. All of a sudden, I was hyperaware of facial expressions, subtle nuances, and hidden feelings that had previously eluded me. After stepping away from the myopic vision of corporate measurements, my perspective broadened to include the complex web of human experience.

How I defined success underwent the most significant transformation. The focus shifted away from accomplishments, material possessions, and praise. It was about creating genuine relationships, living in the now, and making a positive impact on the world while recognizing the worth and potential in every individual I met.

No Longer Behind Glass

As I got on a packed bus for the last time, heading back to the house I'd left six months ago, I reflected on the path that had led me here. Rather than the distance covered or the number of places visited, what truly counted were the lives I had impacted and the wisdom I had gained from my experiences.

I felt like I was swimming in a sea of life, no longer confined by the confines of an aquarium, shielded from the currents but cut off from all its bounty. With a new sense of direction and purpose, I found myself swimming through life's currents like a fish in open water.

Probably never in his lifetime would the young man whose fleeting look at the traffic light start me on this course of action. However, I had begun to view him and everyone else I had encountered during these six months as mentors, with valuable lessons in perseverance, genuineness, and humanity imparted by each.

The lowering light created lengthy shadows across the countryside as the bus wove its way through the downtown streets. Life went outside the window in all its lovely, chaotic craziness. However, at this point, the glass barrier had broken down. Instead of standing on the sidelines, I dove headfirst into the action, immersing myself in the ocean of life.

I had never felt wealthier, even though I had lost money selling my Mercedes.

Chapter 2:
Mumbai Locals: The Pulse of the City

A Different Universe

My first ride on a Mumbai local train was on a wet rainy morning. A momentary break in the rain had left behind a sticky humidity that felt like an unwanted second skin clinging to my flesh. The beautiful morning light filtered through the clouds as I stepped onto the platform at Andheri Station, and little puddles formed as water dripped from the overhanging shelter.

The platform seemed to have a life of its own. There were hundreds, if not thousands, of individuals standing in irregular shapes that looked like lines. Dressed in a wide variety of formal and informal office wear, kurtas, and sarees, they all moved as if in one, yet each garment concealed an unseen story. To liberate their hands, women wearing vibrant sarees tucked their pallus delicately around the waist. Men clad in dress shirts tucked newspapers into the back pockets and rolled up their sleeves. Students at the university stood in clusters, giggling and fiddling with their phones.

It was as if I had stepped into another world, teeming with activity and tales. In my Mercedes, I had driven past this station innumerable times, peered out the tinted windows at this world. But now that I'm standing here, I see how little I really saw.

It astounded me how many people there were. The quantity is important, but what really matters is the rhythm they have, which is like a human tide that ebbs and flows with the arrival and departure of trains. This was the most alien soundscape I'd ever heard: screeching speakers, sellers shouting "chai-chai," and the incessant hum of discussion in a variety of languages, broken only by loud cellphone rings and bursts of laughing.

I waited a moment as the train squealed to a stop. Working in the corporate world had accustomed me to regimented settings, such as air-conditioned vehicles, well-organized meetings, and rigid timetables. Even though everything was chaotic, this place seemed alive, unlike my usual, regimented life.

The Art of Boarding

First with a distant rumble, the oncoming train declared itself then with a blast of warm air pushing along the platform. The doors hadn't even fully opened as it screamed to stop when a flood of commuters shot forward from behind me.

Frozen, not sure what to do. Should I press ahead? Watch for the throng to thin out? *"Naya hai kya? Chalo, aage badho!"* ~ "Are you new? Come on, move forward!"

The momentum of the mob swept me ahead before I could reply. Hands on my back, I felt softly but firmly pushed toward the open door. In seconds, my body pushed against strangers from all sides as I was thrown into a packed compartment. Though curiously grounded, the smells of moist garments, metal, and human sweat were strong. This was the raw, unprocessed scent of humanity—not the cleaned-up scent of workplace air fresheners or automobile perfume.The train jolted ahead, and I almost fell. A middle-aged woman who hardly looked up from her book as she assisted me stretched out to steady me. I caught a ceiling handle, but the unfamiliar pressure in my arm was already hurting.

"Pehli baar local train mein?" ~ "First time on a local train?" asked a voice beside me.

I looked to find a man grinning knowingly. He had seen my distress with the experienced commuter's skilled eye.

"It shows that much?" I answered, trying to change my posture as the train jerked around a bend.

He grinned. "Everyone recalls their initial impression. You will be forcing your way in like you were born doing by next week."

The open windows let in a blast of somewhat cooler air as the train accelerated, offering brief relief from the heat in the packed cabin. Mumbai shone outside in a kaleidoscope of metropolitan India, slums and skyscrapers, temples and stores all bleeding together.

I came to observe the city from inside its rushing arteries, not from above in a high-rise office or from the cocoon of a luxury automobile. This train was the lifeblood of Mumbai itself, not only getting passengers somewhere.

The Dabbawala's Precision

Trying to stay in the packed compartment, I gripped a pole as the train swirled. Beside me was a middle-aged man carrying a big metal rack full of stacked tiffine boxes sporting a Gandhi cap and a dingy white blouse. His body swung in instinctive accord with the train's rhythm, even if it was choppy. He kept perfect equilibrium.

Seeing my inquisitive look, he grinned and remarked, *"Pehli baar?* ~ "First time?"

I nodded, and he chuckled. *"Local mein chadhna aur utarna ek kala hai. Seekh jaoge."* ~ "Getting on and off a local train is an art. You'll learn."

Keshav was a dabbawala who had been delivering lunches all over Mumbai for more than twenty years. His aged face showed the lines of early mornings and long days, but his eyes gleamed with a serene pride.

Keshav told bits of his life as the train rushed toward Churchgate. Every day, he rose up at four a.m. rode to several houses to pick tiffins, then delivered them with mechanical accuracy. By five thirty AM, he had gathered hundreds of lunch boxes from suburban homes, each stamped with a distinct code of colors and symbols.

"Yeh dekhiye," "~ "Look at this," he said, pointing to the markings on the tiffins. *"Yeh hamara GPS hai."* ~ "This is our GPS."

Unreadable to me, the marks were a complicated system of codes denoting routes, destinations, and receivers. Not fancy technology or smartphone apps—just a system created a century ago that still ran perfectly.

"Harvard wale aaye the humein dekhne," ~ "People from Harvard came to study us," he mentioned with obvious but understated pride. *"Unhone kaha ki hamara error rate—galti karne ka chance—ten lakh deliveries mein sirf ek hai."* ~ "They said our error rate—the chance of making a mistake—is just one in a million deliveries."

I had heard about this before—how Harvard Business School had actually looked at the extraordinary accuracy of the Mumbai dabbawalas. But hearing from Keshav and seeing him negotiate the packed train carrying his priceless cargo changed my respect for this particular Mumbai institution.

"Human logon ki pet ka sawaal hai, saab. Galti karinge toh lagegi." ~ "It's about people's hunger, sir. If we make a mistake, someone will go hungry" He expressed this not dramatically but rather as a basic assertion of accountability.

I kept his remarks with me. In a city as large and detached as Mumbai, his obligation toward total strangers was both modest and motivating. He was providing home-cooked meals that linked families split over the great distances of the city, not goods. One tiffrine at a time, he was in his own way piecing Mumbai together.

Dreams in Transit

As I continued down the aisle, leaning against the window, I beheld a young woman who appeared utterly absorbed in a textbook resting on her knees. Her extraordinary composure allowed her to highlight sections and make notes in the margins despite the jostling of the full train.

I was able to get closer to her during a short interval in the trip when several individuals exited. Before getting back to her book, Advanced Financial Management, she took a quick look above.

"Preparing for exams?" "Excuse me?" I inquired.

Looking down, she gave a silent nod. The MBA finals are here. I will be back the following month.

Meera was the name of the girl who made the daily trek from Virar to South Mumbai to attend college. "It's three hours one way," she remarked with a worn-out grin as she brought her book to a close. But there is a scholarship opportunity for my MBA program if I do well. There's no regret.

The intensity of Meera's resolve was evident. Her day began at 4:30 in the morning, she boarded the 5:40 train, and she continued to attend classes until the evening, frequently getting home after 9 in the evening. However, she discussed it casually, as if making such sacrifices was the norm in order to succeed.

"Don't you get tired?" "Excuse me?" I inquired.

"Affirmative", she said. "However, is a choice available?" Opportunities like this did not exist for my parents.

Her working-class parents were banking on her schooling to improve the family's financial status. She was adamant about making good use of the money her parents had to part with from a tiny plot of family land in order to pay for her bachelor's degree.

"My father says, *'Paisa train ke ticket ka nahin, teri sapno ka hai.'*" ~ 'The money spent on train tickets is not for travel but for your dreams.'"

Her strength as a runner was inspiring. She persevered through long commutes and packed trains every day in pursuit of the future she dreamed of for her family. For her, the train was more than simply a means of transportation; it was an investment in her future and a mobile classroom.

While I watched her get back to her studies while more people boarded at the next station, I couldn't help but wonder how she managed to stay focused in those conditions. During my time working for a corporation, I took pride in my work ethic. I would spend long hours in offices that provided me with ergonomic chairs and coffee whenever I wanted it. Hard effort, in Meera's view, is more admirable than mine.

She showed the world that with faith and determination, everything is possible, and her story served as a sobering reminder that privilege is about more than simply money.

A Heart Adrift

The crash decreased significantly as commuters disembarked near Dadar station, commonly termed the heart of Mumbai, where the Western and Central lines intersect. At that moment, I beheld a young man standing by the entrance, his eyes fixed on the passing scenery.

His demeanor was blank, in contrast to the intent looks of other commuters. In contrast to the rest of the lively crowd, he stood out due to his wrinkled clothing, disheveled hair, and distant pain in his eyes.

After he took a seat, I scooted over to take his place. It wasn't until I said, *"Kahan ja rahe ho, bhai?"* ~ "Where are you heading, brother?" that he acknowledged my existence.)

As if roused from a profound contemplation, he abruptly pivoted. He hesitated for a second before finally saying, *"Pata nahi."* ~ "I am uncertain."

For days, a man named Ravi had been lost and alone on local trains. He was employed at a little electronics store in Andheri, but he had been taking the train to and from work, alighting at random stops only when he was too tired or hungry to continue.

"Pyar mein haar gaya, gharwalo ne samjha nahi." ~ "I lost in love, and my family didn't understand."

In fragmented lines, his story unfolded—a secret rendezvous at Marine Drive, a future with a girl from a different caste, and a love affair. Her family set her up for a marriage to someone from their own group the moment they found out about their relationship. Even Ravi's own parents advised him to put her in the past and go on, worried about the consequences and their place in their tight-knit village.

"Lekin sir, jab dil ka har dhadkan kisi ke naam se judi ho, toh bhoolna asaan nahi hota." "But sir, when every heartbeat is tied to someone's name, forgetting isn't easy."

Just as he finished speaking, the train entered the station beyond. Ravi abruptly rose to his feet before completing his thought. *"Yahan utarna hai."* ~ "I must get off at this point."

"However, you mentioned that you were unsure of your destination," I commented, my confusion evident.

His smile was sorrowful. *"Main kabhi bhi, kahin bhi utar jata hoon. Fark nahi padta."* ~ "I get off anywhere, anytime. It doesn't matter."

He exited from the train and joined the throng, a man with no clear objective. Like so many others, I watched as he faded into the crowd, another wanderer in the city of dreams. Society stifles young people's emotions beneath the weight of history and expectation, and it's not because they're weak; rather, it's the other way around.

I couldn't help but wonder, as the train chugged away, how many more people were like Ravi—there physically, but emotionally distant, bearing invisible loads that nobody else could perceive.

The Ticket Collector's Dignity

An unexpected encounter with a transgender woman working as a ticket collector occurred to me at Churchgate Station, the last stop on the Western Line. Seeing someone dressed as a government official was shocking in India, a country where members of the "third gender" group, also known as hijras, endure widespread prejudice and have few job prospects.

Her name was Lata. She sat at her booth with an air of professionalism, checking tickets and issuing fines with remarkable efficiency. I pretended to peruse the station map nearby while I stayed after having my ticket checked, curious about her story.

I went over to her and complimented her on her efficiency when there was a slow period in the flow of passengers.

"Pehli baar dekh rahe ho kya?" ~ "Seeing it for the first time?" she inquired, her expression betraying her real intent.

I expressed my astonishment by nodding.

"Humein bhi normal naukri ka haq hai." ~ "We also have the right to normal jobs." Her voice was firm but not confrontational.

In order to secure this position with the government, Lata had to endure years of prejudice. Everything from bullying and rejection to having doors slammed in her face was detailed on account of the hardships.

"Pehle log humein bheekh maangne par majboor karte the" ~ "Earlier, society forced us to beg," she said, her voice filled with quiet strength. *"Ab main ek izzatdar naukri karti hoon."* "Now, I do a respectable job."

Her smile was wry when I inquired about the way people treat her these days. *"Badalne mein waqt lagega. Abhi bhi log yeh sochte hain ke hijre sirf taali bajake paisa maang sakte hain."* ~ "Change takes time. Even now, people think hijras can only clap and beg for money."

Respect for her dignity was unwavering in the face of persistent bigotry; some people's views on hijras have not changed. In a world that had attempted to disregard her, she demanded respect with every meticulously pressed uniform and expertly executed transaction.

Her narrative strongly affected me. This was a lady battling for more than simply her life; she was fighting for the basic human right to be respected for her abilities and worth. War isn't necessarily fought on battlefields; in fact, some people fight battles daily simply to stay alive.

She reverted to her official tone, arranged her papers, and watched as more passengers poured into her booth. Even after we ended our talk, the lesson she taught me about bravery stuck with me.

The Symphony of Shared Space

Over several weeks of daily travels, I became attuned to the sensory symphony that was the Mumbai local train experience. There was a rhythm to the madness, a method to the chaos that at first had seemed so overwhelming.

The physical sensations were intense and unavoidable. Sweat trickled down my back in the packed compartments, regardless of whether it was raining outside. My shoulders bumped against others with each turn of the track, creating a strange dance of bodies swaying in unconscious unison. The metal handrails became slick with the moisture from hundreds of palms. During peak hours, I often found myself lifted slightly off my feet, carried by the density of bodies rather than standing on my own.

The sounds created a layered soundtrack—the wheels clacking against tracks formed the bass line, while conversations in Marathi, Hindi, Gujarati, and English wove in and out like musical phrases. Vendors somehow squeezed through impossibly tight spaces, their singsong calls of *"vada pav-vada pav"* or *"chai-garam chai"* adding percussion to the arrangement. Occasionally, a group of blind musicians would board, singing devotional songs and collecting donations, their harmonies rising above the mechanical noise.

Most surprising was the camaraderie that emerged in these crowded conditions. Regular commuters recognized each other and saved seats. Small courtesies abounded—a hand extended to help someone board, a bag held while another adjusted their clothing, a shared newspaper, a warning about a station approaching. During monsoon downpours, strangers offered corner spots to those who were drenched.

"Adjust karna Mumbai ka sabse bada talent hai, bhai" ~ “Adjusting is Mumbai's greatest talent, my friend)," a fellow passenger once quipped when I expressed amazement at how many people could fit into a single compartment. The comment drew knowing laughter from everyone within earshot.

This adjustment wasn't just physical—it was a mindset, a city-wide agreement to make space for one another, to endure discomfort collectively rather than demand comfort individually.

In the ladies' compartment (which I observed from adjacent doors during less crowded periods), women shared food, exchanged recipes, minded each other's children, and warned newcomers about lecherous men at particular stations. In the general compartments, politics and cricket were debated vigorously but rarely with animosity. The first-class compartments, despite their higher fare, were hardly less crowded but maintained their own code of behavior—newspapers were shared in silence, and conversations were conducted in hushed tones.

Each compartment was its own ecosystem, its own temporary community dissolved and reformed with each journey. Together, they created a moving mosaic of Mumbai's immense diversity.

Life Lessons on Rails

After weeks of using the train every day, I started to notice the people of Mumbai for more than just cars. Their resiliency, accommodating nature, and boundless energy mirrored that of the metropolis. Being humble and part of a community were the lessons of each ride.

What I discovered about Maslow's hierarchy of needs is that, even in the midst of a crowded train at rush hour, the most basic need is to stay alive; after that, comfort is a luxury; and in the empty gaps, human connection flourishes. I saw several instances of selflessness, such as children offering up their seats to the elderly, complete strangers helping moms arrange their sarees by holding their baby, and passengers forming human chains to help late-runners catch departing trains.

As I looked about, I saw individuals making the most of their space and time. I saw kids studying, professionals going over presentations, and ladies slicing veggies for dinner while balanced on tiffin boxes. There is not a single second that goes underused.

I witnessed the heartless callousness of city life—how a sick person would be given room and help the second they were sick, but the same mob would rush forward impatiently a few minutes later. Regardless of the terrible frequency of accidents or the torrential rains that swamped the tracks, the trains would continue to run. Stopping would have been too costly for the city and the trains.

The ability of Mumbaikars to persevere through adversity, to find happiness despite setbacks, and to make meaningful connections in brief interactions was what really stood out to me. Every story showed a distinct side of human perseverance and ambition, whether it was the dabbawala's commitment, the student's hopes, the young man's grief, or the ticket collector's pride.

From Observer to Participant

On my last planned ride on the Mumbai locals, I found myself standing near the door as the train pulled into Churchgate Station. Weeks earlier, I had been hesitant, overwhelmed by the crush of humanity, unsure of the unwritten rules of this complex ecosystem.

Now, I moved with confidence, my body instinctively leaning into the turns, my hand knowing exactly when to grip tighter on the handrail, my feet finding stable positions without conscious thought. Without realizing it, I had become part of this daily ritual—no longer an observer but a participant.

As I stepped off onto the platform, drenched in sweat but filled with a profound sense of connection, a young man stumbled beside me, clearly new to the Mumbai local experience. I steadied him with a hand on his shoulder.

"Pehli baar?" ~ "First time?" I asked, echoing the question that had been posed to me weeks ago.

He nodded, looking slightly overwhelmed.

"Local mein chadhna aur utarna ek kala hai. Seekh jaoge." ~ "Getting on and off a local train is an art. You'll learn."

As I walked away, I realized that these daily journeys had transformed me. The Mumbai locals, with all their chaos and charm, had become my classroom, teaching me lessons no boardroom could ever offer. I had entered as an outsider, a corporate executive playing at common life. I was leaving as just another Mumbaikar—shaped by the rhythm of the rails, connected to the city's pulse in ways I never could have been from behind the tinted windows of my Mercedes.

The wealth I had gained couldn't be measured in conventional terms. It was the richness of experience, the depth of understanding, the breadth of human connection. I had sold my Mercedes at a loss, but in the crowded compartments of Mumbai's local trains, I had found treasures of far greater value.

Chapter 3:
Delhi's Streets: Chaos, Charm, and Conversations

A City of Contrasts

Duality was the first thing that jumped out at me when I arrived in Delhi. The city's unique blend of old and new, beautiful and chaotic, whispers of history and roars of modern ambition created an environment where contrast flourished.

Crammed but interconnected, Mumbai had felt like one metropolitan flow. On the other hand, Delhi appeared to occupy more than one era at once. In an instant, I was in the immaculate grounds of Lutyens' Delhi, gazing in awe at the colonial-era buildings set amid broad, tree-lined roads and meticulously groomed gardens. The following day, I found myself bewildered by the winding alleys of Old Delhi, where buildings that were hundreds of years old leaned on each other like long-lost friends confiding in each other.

The individuals were also markedly different. A ragged-shirted cycle rickshaw puller would skillfully weave around a shiny luxury vehicle on the same roadway. People selling vegetables had calloused hands that had never been rested, and women in designer attire with expensive handbags would bargain with them. In the shadow of the glass buildings housing international firms, barefoot youngsters would play cricket with wooden crates for wickets.

My cab driver had made the comment, "Delhi is not a city," when I was first dropped off. "It is many cities stacked on top of each other, fighting for the same space."

After the rigorous pace of Mumbai, the beat of Delhi felt different—just as intense, but with more contradiction, more argumentation, and more dramatic extremes. Delhi was a complicated raga with sudden peaks and valleys, peaceful beauty interspersed with shocking dissonance, in contrast to Mumbai's relentlessly quick melody.

The notorious air pollution in Delhi was at its worst when I came in the winter. Over the metropolis, a misty shroud lowered its harsh edges while simultaneously serving as a continual sobering reminder of the cost of advancement. Ancient landmarks and contemporary architecture were bathed in an ethereal light as the morning sun shone through the haze like a pale orange disk.

Into the Heart of Old Delhi

Chandni Chowk, one of Delhi's oldest and busiest markets, was the starting point of my exploration of the city's core. I got there in the late afternoon, just as the sun was setting and painting the medieval streets in a beautiful golden light. Regardless of the pollution, the way the light danced through the alleys and illuminated the dust particles as they floated like little stars was inherently romantic.

Everything around me went into hyperdrive the second I got off the subway at Chandni Chowk. The aroma was the first thing that caught my attention. It was a complex blend of scents, like jalebi frying in huge iron kadhais, pickles sold in open barrels, the earthy scent of freshly ground spices at shops that were over a century old, and the promise of savory bread baking in tandoors.

A lovely cacophony of voices yelling out in English, Punjabi, Urdu, and Hindi followed. Shopkeepers used their charm to entice potential customers: "Arrey bhaiya, idhar dekhiye, special price sirf aapke liye!" ("Hey, look here, a special price just for you!" he said to his brother). The sellers' singsong cadences swelled and rolled like the waves as they declared their wares. There was a tense cacophony of rickshaw bells, occasionally drowned out by the honk of auto-rickshaws that had managed to sneak into pedestrian-only roads.

Shopkeepers arranged colorful textiles outside their shops, laborers balanced impossibly large bundles on top of their heads, brides-to-be carefully examined jewelry, tourists clutched cameras and maps, and locals navigated the crowds with the practiced ease of creatures born to this beautiful chaos. The streets were a vibrant blur of humanity.

It was both thrilling and terrifying. I thought I was used to city crowds after spending weeks in Mumbai, but the Old City of Delhi offered a new type of density—one steeped with centuries of history, tradition, and almost rebellious endurance.

The Poet on the Rickshaw

I felt lost as I meandered through the winding streets, pausing every so often to admire complex silver jewelry or see deft hands spinning *roomali rotis* that were so thin you could see a newspaper through them. Here, the streets wound and turned in ways that had been laid down hundreds of years ago, rendering the maps on my phone completely worthless.

Jama Masjid, a stunning mosque that attested to the Mughal majesty, was my destination after hailing a cycle rickshaw from Chandni Chowk. The thin man who pulled the rickshaw had a weathered face and calloused hands from decades of hard work. The gray in his beard gave him away as being in his late fifties, but he walked with the energy of a man half his age.

He looked me up and down and said, "Jama Masjid?" for sure. "Twenty minutes in this traffic. Fifty rupees."

I gave the signal and got on board. I watched his deft motions as he started pedaling, weaving among crowds I hadn't even noticed were there. The consequence of years of personal understanding of these routes, every pedal turn and direction adjustment looked deliberate yet natural.

He seemed to sense my astonishment and questioned, "First time in Delhi?" from behind me.

"This is my first time seeing authentic Delhi," I responded. "I've been here before, but always in cars with drivers, going from one air-conditioned building to another."

His laughter filled the air. Then, sir, you have never laid eyes on Delhi. No one in Delhi calls a building home. Streets are where Delhi comes to life.

For almost fifteen years, a man named Iqbal had pulled a rickshaw. His previous experience was in the construction industry, where he contributed to the edifice of the glass skyscrapers that now grace the city's skyline.

Amidst apparent physical fatigue, he spoke with a smile, *"Dilli ki sadke toh apni jaan hain, sahab"* ~ "The streets of Delhi are my life, sir". As we navigated the crowded streets, he filled me in on his story of how, as a teenager, he had escaped from a small hamlet in Bihar, seeking employment and a future that was as big as his desires, despite his meager resources.

"Kabhi socha tha ki bada aadmi banunga, koi dukan kholunga, par ab yeh cycle hi meri duniya hai." "I once dreamt of

becoming a successful man, opening my own shop, but now this cycle is my world," he said without self-pity.

The lyricism of his words was the most surprising thing to me. Iqbal had the kind of eloquence that many college professors would envy, despite his lack of formal education. His face brightened as I brought this up.

Evidently pleased, he added, *"Aap pehle aadmi hain jo meri baat mein kavita sunte hain"* "You're the first person who hears poetry in my words," he said, visibly pleased. *"Main likhta bhi hoon, jab waqt milta hai."* ~ "I write too, when I find time."

As we neared the majestic steps of Jama Masjid, he spoke a few words of his own work in response to my expression of interest:

"Jo raat ko chhupa diya, subah ne wahi dikhaya,

Jo dilli ne chhupa diya, dilli ne wahi bataya."

~ "What the night concealed was exposed by the morning,

What Delhi attempted to conceal was disclosed by Delhi itself."

His words astounded me with their profundity and simplicity. Here was a man whose aspirations from his boyhood had been crushed by the incessant pressures of economic need; he had been consumed by the metropolis. Even though his job was mundane, he managed to find beauty in it and turn it into poetry.

"What does your poem mean to you?" As we came to a halt at the mosque's magnificent entryway, I inquired.

"It means that Delhi is honest in its dishonesty," he replied with a philosophical smile. "It promises dreams it cannot fulfill, but it never hides the reality of life. The struggle is visible everywhere if you choose to see it. And in that truth, there is a kind of beauty."

I pondered, as I paid him—far more than he had asked, but I knew better than to pass it off as charity—how many more artists, thinkers, and dreamers lurked beneath the surface of this city's drivers, sellers, and laborers.

Tea and Truth with a Forgotten Soldier

As dusk drew near, I had spent hours exploring the Jama Masjid and the surrounding marketplaces and was now at India Gate. As the sky grew darker, the perpetual flame of the iconic war memorial stood as a solemn reminder of the sacrifices made for the nation's freedom.

Families were out in full force, relishing the evening breeze on the expansive lawns that encircled the monument. There were merchants selling roasted peanuts, ice cream, and LED-lit children's toys, while youngsters flew colorful kites and young couples sat closely together on the grass.

I paused at a little tea cart situated next to one of the paths since I was exhausted from walking. At an improvised counter, encircled by plain wooden seats, a child boiled kettles of tea over a gas stove. In the middle of the city, a sensory paradise emerged as the fragrant milk, cardamom, and ginger simmered to perfection.

Sitting alone, I spotted an old man who appeared to be seeing more than just a monument as he stared intently at India Gate as I took a seat. As he raised his cup to his lips, his hands quivered a little, giving the impression that his physique was fragile, despite his time-honed features. His posture—a certain straightness of the back, a particular way of holding his shoulders—spoke of discipline and command, even though his clothes were basic.

The tea vendor leaned over and whispered to me, *"Fauji hain. Colonel sahab. Roz shaam ko aate hain."* ~ "He's an army man. A Colonel. Comes every evening."

I was struck by the old soldier's silent watch. Gathering my tea, I made my way over to him. "May I join you, sir?"

After a brief surprised glance upward, he pointed to the vacant seat on the bench. His wrinkled face showed the signs of someone who had endured tough experiences, as I got closer. He had a lengthy scar that began on his right cheek and faded into his pepper and salt beard.

"Aap bhi fauji hain?" ~ "Are you also serving in the military?" he said, his voice exuding the air of someone accustomed to commanding respect.

"No, sir. Just a civilian attempting to gain a better understanding of my country," I responded.

His name was Colonel Rana, and he was a veteran of many wars, including the Kargil War. He had a modest apartment in East Delhi by himself after retiring. His wife had died, his children had moved away, and most of his friends and acquaintances had long since disappeared.

"So why do you come here every evening?" I pointed to India Gate and asked.

He sipped his drink deliberately and remained silent for a long period. His voice was low and emotionally agitated when he finally spoke.

"Aapne desh ke liye ladayi ladi, sir. Kaisa lagta hai yahaan aake?" (You fought for the country, sir. How does it feel to be here now?) I asked.

He gave a small, bitter smile. "Jung ladne wale log kabhi retire nahi hote. Bas bhool diye jaate hain." (People who fight wars never retire. They are just forgotten.)

His remarks struck me like a fist. Unrecognized, he sat with his evening tea and memories of the man who had risked his life for the nation. Even though the living manifestations of sacrifices were meant to be honored by the perpetual light at India Gate, they often sank into obscurity.

"Mujhe tankhawa nahi chahiye thi, bas izzat chahiye thi" ~ "I didn't need a salary, I just wanted respect," he said, his gaze remaining locked on the monument. "But people remember soldiers only on Independence Day and Republic Day. The rest of the year, we are invisible."

India Gate was illuminated by the surrounding lights as night set, casting a warm golden light upon the monument. Colonel Rana completed his cup, got to his feet (aided by a cane that I had missed), and got ready to go.

How about tomorrow? I wanted to know.

He stated, "Where else would I go?" in response. "My friends are here." He then made a motion toward the memorial's engraved names.

As he made his way away, I could see him disappearing into the nighttime crowd. I pondered how heartless a culture must be that honors its soldiers in theory but disregards their physical bodies.

The Question That Had No Answer

My exploration of Delhi continued over the next few weeks, taking me from the academic corridors of Delhi University to the diplomatic enclaves of Chanakyapuri, from the spiritual solace of Nizamuddin Dargah to the consumer paradise of malls in Saket.

One evening, as I wandered through the modernized surroundings of Connaught Place with its colonial architecture now housing international brand outlets, I encountered a different kind of reality. Amid the well-dressed shoppers and tourists, a group of hijras (transgender individuals) moved through the crowd, their approach announced by the traditional clapping of hands.

In Indian society, hijras occupy a paradoxical position—revered for their supposed power to bless or curse, yet marginalized in everyday life. Dressed in bright sarees, wearing heavy makeup and distinctive jewelry, they are hard to miss, yet many passersby studiously avoided eye contact.

One of them, taller than the rest and with striking features accentuated by bold makeup, approached me directly. Unlike the others who were asking for money more aggressively, she simply stood before me, her eyes questioning.

"Aap humse baat karenge?" ~ "Will you talk to me?" she asked, seeming surprised when I didn't immediately look away.

Her name was Sangeeta, and she had been living with her hijra community since the age of twelve, when her family had discovered her gender identity and forced her to leave home. While others in her group continued to approach people for money, she sat with me on a bench and shared her story with a quiet dignity that belied her flamboyant appearance.

"Agar izzat wali naukri milti, toh yeh kaam kyun karti?" ~ "If I could get a respectable job, why would I do this?" she said when I asked about her life on the streets.

For hijras like Sangeeta, options were severely limited. Traditional society shunned them, and despite recent legal recognition of the "third gender," practical discrimination remained rampant. Most doors of conventional employment remained firmly closed.

"Hamare liye sirf do raste hain—ya toh sadak pe bheekh maango, ya naach-gaana karo." ~ "For us, there are only two paths—either beg on the streets or dance and sing for money."

What struck me most deeply was a philosophical question she posed, her eyes filling with tears as she spoke:

"Log kehte hain bhagwan ne hume alag banaya. Toh bhagwan ne phir hamare liye jagah kyun nahi banayi?" ~ "People say God made us different. Then why didn't He make a place for us?"

That question haunted me. Why do we push people into the shadows, and then judge them for living there? How can a society that prides itself on inclusiveness and diversity be so selective about which differences it accepts?

As the evening crowd swirled around us—shoppers with branded bags, couples heading to restaurants, executives leaving their offices—Sangeeta seemed simultaneously part of this urban landscape and completely separate from it. Visible yet invisible. Present yet excluded.

Before she left to rejoin her group, she pressed a small jasmine flower into my palm. "For listening," she said simply. "Not many do."

The City of a Thousand Stories

Delhi, I came to realize, was not just a city—it was an emotion, a contradiction, a never-ending battle between struggle and ambition. If Mumbai was defined by its resilience, Delhi was characterized by its stark contrasts and unapologetic honesty about those contrasts.

Here, you could find dreamers like Iqbal, the rickshaw puller whose poetic soul survived decades of physical labor.

You could encounter forgotten heroes like Colonel Rana, who had given everything for his country only to be left with memories and a daily pilgrimage to a monument. You could meet people like Sangeeta, navigating a society that had no comfortable place for them yet somehow maintaining dignity and philosophical depth despite daily humiliation.

In the same day, you could witness unimaginable wealth in the farmhouses of Chhatarpur and grinding poverty in the slums of Seemapuri. You could hear classical music performances in India Habitat Centre and the latest Bollywood hits blaring from roadside stalls. You could taste the most refined cuisine in five-star hotels and the most authentic flavors from street vendors whose recipes had been perfected over generations.

This complexity was reflected in Delhi's physical landscape as well—ancient tombs stood next to modern apartment complexes, medieval forts overlooked metro stations, sacred rivers flowed past industrial zones. Somehow, all these contradictions coexisted not in harmony but in a dynamic tension that gave the city its unique energy.

As my time in Delhi drew to a close, I found myself standing on a pedestrian overbridge near Connaught Place during the evening rush hour. Below me, the traffic moved in organized chaos—cars, motorcycles, auto-rickshaws, and buses weaving around each other in patterns that seemed to follow some unwritten choreography. The setting sun cast long shadows across the colonial-era buildings, while office workers hurried home, street vendors packed up their wares, and the city prepared for its transformation into its nocturnal avatar.

From this vantage point, I could see both the beauty and brutality of urban India—the resourcefulness that allowed millions to coexist in limited space, the injustices that determined who rode in cars and who pulled them, the resilience that kept people moving forward despite overwhelming challenges, and the dreams that brought people from villages to this urban behemoth in search of better lives.

Delhi had shown me that poverty and wealth, kindness and cruelty, tradition and modernity could exist side by side without reconciliation. It had taught me that beauty could be found in contradictions and wisdom in unexpected places. It had reminded me that behind each face was a story as complex and worthy of attention as my own.

As I descended from the overbridge and merged back into the human tide, I carried with me Iqbal's poetry, Colonel Rana's forgotten sacrifice, and Sangeeta's unanswerable question. Delhi had not offered me solutions or comfort. Instead, it had given me something far more valuable—a deeper understanding of the magnificent complexity of human existence.

And perhaps that was the greatest wealth of all.

Chapter 4:
Chennai: of Autos, Temples, and Tea Stalls

A Different Kind of Heat

Chennai greeted me with an embrace of heat unlike anything I had experienced in Mumbai or Delhi. If Mumbai's humidity was clingy and desperate, Chennai's heat was confident and deliberate— a steady presence that settled on your skin and stayed there. It wasn't just hot; it was deeply, profoundly hot, as if the sun had developed a personal interest in the city and decided to hover a little closer to its streets.

As I stepped out of Chennai Central Railway Station, the midday heat hit me like a physical force. The air shimmered above the pavement, and I could feel sweat forming instantly on my forehead, back, and chest. But there was something else in that heat— a stillness, a certain unhurried quality that seemed to permeate the city itself.

The sensory landscape around me unfolded gradually. The roar of auto-rickshaws, their yellow-and-black bodies swarming around the station exit, created a constant backdrop of sound punctuated by short, sharp honks. Street vendors called out in melodious Tamil, a language whose musicality made even commerce sound like poetry to my untrained ears. The aroma of filter coffee wafted from a small stall nearby, rich and inviting, promising brief respite from the heat.

In the distance, despite being miles away, I could sense rather than smell the sea— a certain quality to the air, a hint of salt in the breeze that occasionally cut through the heat like a merciful whisper. Chennai, I realized, was a city caught between land and ocean, between ancient tradition and reluctant modernity, and between fiery heat and cooling breeze.

Unlike the immediately overwhelming chaos of Mumbai or the stark contrasts of Delhi, Chennai revealed itself slowly, deliberately—a city that didn't feel the need to announce itself loudly but rather waited for you to pay attention to its quieter rhythms.

The Philosophy of Auto Driving

"Where to, sir?" asked an auto driver, pulling up beside me as I stood pondering my next move. His face was lean and weathered, with sharp, observant eyes that crinkled at the corners when he smiled.

"Mount Road area," I replied, naming the street where I had booked accommodation.

He nodded and gestured for me to get in. Unlike in Delhi, where lengthy negotiations would precede any journey, he simply turned on the meter—a practice I would learn was common in Chennai, where auto drivers largely followed regulations despite tourists' expectations to the contrary.

As I settled into the back seat, the driver introduced himself as Arul. "First time in Chennai?" he asked, glancing at me in his rearview mirror.

"Yes," I admitted.

"Then you hold tight," he grinned. "Chennai auto ride is special education."

That was my only warning before Arul launched his vehicle into the traffic with a sudden acceleration that pushed me back against the seat. What followed was a masterclass in what I can only describe as automotive ballet— a dance of near-misses, split-second decisions, and instinctive navigation that seemed to defy physics and probability.

Arul weaved through gaps that appeared non-existent until the moment his auto passed through them. He anticipated other vehicles' movements before they showed any indication of turning or stopping. He slowed down or sped up with a rhythm that seemed connected to some invisible traffic pulse only he could detect.

Yet despite what appeared to be a death-defying journey, I gradually realized there was a method to his apparent madness. Arul wasn't reckless; he was fluent in the unwritten language of Chennai traffic. His driving wasn't chaotic— it was adaptive, responsive, almost elegant in its efficiency.

"Saar, this Chennai traffic is like family—always arguing, never going anywhere," he joked, eliciting a nervous laugh from me as he squeezed between a bus and a construction barrier with inches to spare.

As my initial fear subsided, I began to ask him about his life. Arul had been driving an auto for over 15 years, a job he had inherited from his father. Born in a small village near Madurai, he had come to Chennai as a teenager with dreams of working in the film industry.

"I wanted to be a camera assistant," he said, his voice holding no bitterness. "But life had other plans. My father fell sick, so I took his auto. Family first, dreams second— this is our way."

What struck me about Arul wasn't his thwarted ambition but rather how he had transformed necessity into virtue. He spoke of his work with pride, pointing out landmarks as we passed them, explaining the city's geography with the expertise of someone who had internalized every street and shortcut.

"In Chennai auto, you not just get ride," he said, skillfully avoiding a sudden crossing by a cow adorned with garlands. "You get professor of city knowledge!"

The Dream of Filter Coffee

As we navigated through the busy streets, Arul shared his current dream with unexpected eloquence.

"Now I am saving to open small tea kadai," he said, using the Tamil word for shop. "Not a big fancy place with AC and all. Just a simple, clean shop where people can drink real filter coffee, not instant powder nonsense."

He described his vision with such vivid detail that I could almost see it materializing in the heat-hazed air before us. It would have a narrow entrance with a blue door, three small tables inside, and a counter where he would personally prepare the coffee. The walls would be painted cream with photographs of old Chennai. There would be a small shrine in one corner with a picture of his parents and a statue of Ganesha, the remover of obstacles.

"The Best location is near a college or office," he continued, his eyes brightening as he spoke. "Morning time, people want good coffee before work. In the evening, friends meet to discuss politics, cricket, life problems. My shop will give them place for all this."

What fascinated me most was how he described the sensory experience his shop would offer—the rich aroma of freshly ground coffee beans, the rhythmic sound of the traditional brass coffee filter dripping its dark decoction, the satisfying clink of the dabarah-tumbler sets (the traditional stainless-steel vessels for serving South Indian coffee).

"Coffee must have a perfect milk-to-decoction ratio," he explained seriously. "Too much milk, no taste. Too much decoction, too bitter. Balance is everything—in coffee and in life."

As Arul spoke, I realized how narrow my own perspective had been. In my corporate life, I had often discussed business plans involving millions of dollars, international expansion strategies, and market domination. Yet here was a man whose dream—modest by those standards—was articulated with equal passion, equal attention to detail, and perhaps greater personal meaning.

"How much more do you need to save?" I asked.

He thought for a moment. "Two more years, if God willing. Auto is rented now. Once I own it outright, saving will be faster."

"And what will you call your shop?"

His face broke into a wide smile. "Arul's Filter Kaapi Corner—where every cup tells a story."

By the time we reached my destination, I felt I had gained not just a glimpse into one man's life but a new perspective on dreams themselves—how they adapt to circumstances without diminishing in value, how they sustain people through daily struggles, and how their worth isn't measured by their scale but by the meaning they hold for the dreamer.

Life Lessons at a Tea Stall

After settling into my modest lodging, I ventured out in the late afternoon when the worst of the day's heat had begun to subside. Following Arul's recommendation, I sought out a small roadside tea stall near Mylapore, an area known for its ancient temple and traditional Tamil culture.

The stall was nothing more than a thatched roof supported by bamboo poles, sheltering a small counter equipped with a gas stove, several steel containers, and neatly stacked glasses and plates. Behind the counter stood a stout man with a bushy mustache and forearms corded with muscle from years of tea-making. This was Murugan "Anna" (elder brother), as everyone addressed him.

What caught my attention immediately was the theatrical way he prepared coffee. He would pour the dark decoction and boiled milk back and forth between two steel vessels, creating a perfect arc in the air without spilling a drop. This process, I would learn, was called "pulling" the coffee—aerating it to create the perfect frothy texture while cooling it to drinking temperature.

When my turn came, I requested a coffee and watched, mesmerized, as he performed this ritual with practiced precision. The finished coffee, served in a small steel tumbler nestled inside a wider dabarah, was aromatic and perfectly balanced—strong without being bitter, sweet without being cloying.

As I sipped the delicious brew, I noticed how Murugan greeted each customer—from laborers in work clothes to office employees in crisp shirts, from college students to elderly neighborhood residents. He seemed to know not just their beverage preferences but also their lives, asking after family members by name or commenting on recent events in their lives.

"Anna, you must know everyone in this neighborhood," I commented when there was a brief lull in customers.

He wiped his hands on a cloth tucked into his waist and smiled. "Oh yes, sir. But you know, I don't just serve them coffee. I serve them the moment of peace in busy days."

He explained that many of his customers came to his stall not just for refreshment but for brief respite from their daily pressures. For some, it was the only quiet moment in a day filled with work and family responsibilities.

"From rich businessmen to wandering sadhus, everyone comes for tea," he said with a grin, wiping the counter with practiced swipes. "And they all leave their stories here."

I asked him if he ever got tired of listening to people's woes and triumphs.

He laughed, his belly shaking. "Life is like filter coffee, saar. Some days it is too sweet, some days too bitter. But you must drink it all to truly understand it."

As we spoke, the stall bustled with life—a young woman in a saree holding a crying baby approached, and Murugan handed her an extra biscuit, free of charge. "For the little one," he said with a wink. His small gesture of kindness was a reminder that even the simplest interactions could ripple outward, touching lives in ways we might never fully appreciate.

Murugan's wisdom, delivered without pretension between serving customers and washing glasses, stayed with me long after I left his stall. His metaphor about coffee captured something essential about Chennai itself—a city that embraced life's contradictions with quiet acceptance rather than resistance.

The Night Watchman's Solitude

As evening fell, I found myself drawn to Marina Beach, one of the world's longest urban beaches. The seafront provided welcome relief from the city's heat, with a steady breeze carrying the scent of salt and the distant sound of waves breaking on the shore.

The beach was transforming from its daytime identity as a bustling playground to a more contemplative nighttime space. Food vendors lit their stalls, creating pools of golden light that punctuated the growing darkness. Families strolled along the water's edge, children still running and playing despite the late hour. Couples sat on the sand; their silhouettes outlined against the darkening horizon.

Away from the more populated areas, I noticed a solitary figure—an elderly man sitting on a plastic chair outside a row of shuttered beach shops. He wore a khaki uniform and held a wooden staff across his lap, his weathered face illuminated by a single bulb hanging above the shop entrance.

Something about his solitude amid the distant crowd drew me toward him. As I approached, he straightened slightly, assessing whether I represented potential trouble.

"Just taking a walk," I said with a smile, raising my empty hands to indicate my harmlessness.

He relaxed and nodded, gesturing to a stack of plastic chairs beside him. "Sit if you want. The breeze is good tonight."

His name was Ganesan, and he had been working as a night watchman for nearly two decades. Before that, he had worked in various jobs—construction, factory work, and even a brief stint as a movie theater usher. His English was halting but expressive, punctuated with Tamil phrases when words failed him.

"I used to work in the mills," he said, his voice low and steady. "But when they closed, I took this job. It is lonely, saar, but the stars keep me company."

As our conversation deepened, Ganesan spoke of his village near Thanjavur, a place famous for its ancient temple and rich agricultural traditions. His eyes lit up as he described the green fields of his childhood, the temple festivals that brought the entire community together, and the simple yet fulfilling rhythm of rural life.

"I came to Chennai thinking it would be for two years," he said, looking out toward the dark sea. "That was forty years ago."

He had arrived as a young man of twenty, full of dreams and ambitions. He had planned to earn money in the city, send some home to his family, and eventually return to buy land and settle in his village. But life had unfolded differently. He married a woman from the city, had children who grew up as urban dwellers with no connection to village life, and found himself gradually transformed into a person who no longer quite fit in his birthplace.

"Now when I go to the village, they call me 'Chennai-karan' (Chennai man)," he said with a sad smile. "But here in the city, people still hear my accent and call me 'graamathukaran' (village man). I belong nowhere."

This poignant insight struck me deeply. Ganesan existed in a liminal space—not fully accepted in either the world he had left or the world he had adopted. His story reflected the experience of millions of migrants across India who leave their homes seeking better opportunities, only to find themselves caught between identities, belonging fully to neither their past nor their present.

Yet despite this melancholy reflection, there was a quiet dignity to Ganesan. He recited snippets of Tamil poetry, his eyes lighting up with pride as he translated a verse for me: "Even the smallest blade of grass has its place under the sun."

In his words, I found both wisdom and melancholy—a reminder of the resilience that allowed him to find beauty even in the shadows of his solitude.

The Temple's Timeless Rhythms

The following morning, I visited Kapaleeshwarar Temple, one of Chennai's oldest and most revered places of worship. Dating back to the 7th century and rebuilt in the 16th, the temple stands as a testament to the city's deep spiritual roots and architectural heritage.

Even before entering, I was struck by the magnificent gopuram (entrance tower) rising above the surrounding buildings, its pyramidal form covered with intricate sculptures of deities, painted in vibrant colors that somehow withstood the elements. As I approached barefoot, the hot stone underfoot connecting me physically to the earth, I was enveloped in a sensory experience unlike any other.

The sounds came first—the rhythmic chanting of priests, the ringing of bells, devotees murmuring prayers, and the occasional burst of laughter from children playing in the temple courtyard. Then the scents—incense smoke creating fragrant clouds, jasmine flowers strung into garlands, camphor burning in small lamps, and the distinct aroma of ghee used in rituals.

The visual richness was overwhelming—colorful silk-clad deities adorned with flowers and jewelry, intricate carvings telling ancient stories on every pillar and wall, oil lamps creating dancing shadows, and the diverse devotees themselves—from elderly women in traditional nine-yard sarees to young professionals stopping by on their way to offices.

Near the entrance to the inner sanctum, I noticed a woman selling flower garlands and offerings. Her hands moved with remarkable dexterity, stringing jasmine buds and rose petals into elegant patterns with a speed that made it look effortless. Despite the heat, which was becoming increasingly intense as the morning progressed, she worked without pause, her fingers never hesitating.

I purchased a small garland from her and asked how long she had been selling flowers at the temple.

"All my life," she replied simply. "Before me, my mother, and before her, my grandmother."

Her name was Lakshmi, and she had been coming to this same spot outside the temple every day for over thirty years. She would wake before dawn to purchase flowers at the wholesale market, then spend hours creating her garlands and arrangements before taking up her position at the temple by 6 AM.

"Don't your hands get tired?" I asked, watching her thread a needle through delicate jasmine buds without even looking at her work.

She smiled. "Saar, the body may feel tired, but the mind stays peaceful here. The temple gives strength."

What struck me about Lakshmi was not just her skill but her absolute certainty. In a world of constant change, market volatility, and shifting priorities, she embodied an unshakable faith in her purpose. While I had spent years in corporate boardrooms discussing uncertain futures and contingency plans, she approached each day with clear, unwavering focus.

"Do you ever worry about competition? Or changes that might affect your business?" I asked, thinking of how digital disruption had transformed so many traditional trades.

She looked at me with genuine puzzlement. "The temple has stood for centuries. People will always bring flowers to God. What is there to worry about?"

Her faith-centered perspective wasn't naïve; it was profoundly liberating. In the corporate world, I had been taught to anticipate threats, analyze competitors, and constantly adapt to changing market conditions. Lakshmi operated from a different paradigm entirely—one rooted in tradition, devotion, and an acceptance of life's natural rhythms.

As I placed my small jasmine garland before the deity and stood amid the press of devotees waiting for a glimpse of the divine, I felt a momentary connection to something timeless. Here, in this ancient space, concerns about quarterly targets, market shares, and career advancement seemed not just unimportant but almost laughably insignificant.

The Quiet Strength of Chennai

On my final evening in Chennai, I took a long walk through the city as the sun began its descent. The harsh daytime heat had given way to a gentler warmth, and the streets took on a golden glow that softened their edges. I walked without a specific destination, allowing the city to reveal itself at its own pace.

What struck me most was the quality of silence that existed even amid urban activity. Unlike Mumbai's constant cacophony or Delhi's argumentative energy, Chennai possessed a certain restraint—a measured approach to expression that valued substance over volume.

I passed a group of schoolgirls in neat uniforms reciting classical Tamil poetry under a banyan tree, their voices rising and falling in perfect unison. I watched an elderly man perform his yoga routine in a small park, his movements deliberate and precise despite his advanced age. I observed office workers heading home, their conversations conducted in low, thoughtful tones rather than the animated debates I had grown accustomed to in Delhi.

Even the traffic, though considerable, seemed to move with less honking and more patience than in other cities. The buses were crowded but orderly; the pedestrians were purposeful but unhurried.

As darkness fell, I found myself near a small neighborhood temple where evening prayers were beginning. The sound of bells and chanting carried on the sea breeze, creating a soundtrack that seemed to both emerge from and blend back into the city itself. Nearby, a group of men played carrom on a roadside board, their concentration unbroken by the passing traffic. A woman swept the area in front of her house, creating patterns in the dust with her broom.

These ordinary moments, witnessed in the gathering twilight, revealed Chennai's essential character to me. This was a city that didn't shout its struggles but carried them with quiet dignity. It was a place where tradition wasn't a museum piece but a living, breathing framework that gave structure and meaning to daily life.

The corporate world I had left behind valued assertiveness, disruption, and constant reinvention. Chennai offered a different kind of strength—one based on continuity, resilience, and a deep-rooted sense of identity. Neither approach was inherently superior, but experiencing the contrast helped me understand that there are many valid ways to navigate the complexities of modern existence.

As I walked back to my lodging, the evening air now pleasantly cool against my skin, I reflected on all I had experienced—Arul's passionate dream of a coffee shop,

Murugan's philosophical approach to serving tea, Ganesan's melancholy wisdom, and Lakshmi's unshakable faith.

Each of them had taught me something important about life's essential questions: How do we find meaning in our work? How do we maintain dignity amid struggle? How do we balance ambition with acceptance? Where do we truly belong?

Chennai hadn't given me definitive answers to these questions. Instead, it had shown me that the search itself—conducted with patience, reflection, and openness—was what mattered. In its unhurried rhythms and quiet strength, the city had offered me a different model of how to exist in the world—not striving constantly for more, but finding depth and value in what already is.

As the distant sound of temple bells faded into the night, I carried with me not just memories of Chennai but a new appreciation for the power of quietness, the wisdom of tradition, and the profound dignity of lives lived without fanfare but with deep integrity.

Chennai had not shouted its lessons at me. It had simply lived them, trusting that I would pay attention.

Chapter 5:
Bangalore: Startups, Struggles, and Shared Autos

A City of Contrasting Realities

Bangalore—or Bengaluru, as it has been officially known since 2014—greeted me with weather that felt like a gift after Chennai's relentless heat. A pleasant breeze carried the scent of flowering trees as I stepped out of the railway station, and the air held a crispness that instantly lit my mood. This city, perched at over 3,000 feet above sea level on the Deccan Plateau, enjoys a climate that has drawn people here for generations—first as a retirement haven, then as a military cantonment, and now as India's Silicon Valley.

The city's transformation from "Garden City" to "Tech Hub" was immediately visible. Gleaming glass towers housing multinational corporations rose alongside colonial-era bungalows and traditional markets. Young professionals in smart casual attire hurried along streets where fruit vendors still pushed wooden carts. Coffee shops serving espresso and avocado toast operated next to traditional darshinis offering steaming idlis and filter coffee at a fraction of the price.

But as I would soon discover, beneath Bangalore's reputation as India's most cosmopolitan and forward-looking city lay contradictions and struggles invisible to the casual observer. The technology boom that had transformed the city's skyline and economy had also created new fault lines—between tradition and innovation, security and risk, the privileged tech workforce and those hustling on the margins of the digital economy.

I was eager to explore these contradictions, to understand what happened when ancient Indian traditions collided with cutting-edge innovation. After settling into my modest accommodation in Indiranagar—an area that perfectly represented Bangalore's dual personality with its mix of old homes and trendy restaurants—I set out to explore the city not through its tourist attractions, but through the lives of its people.

The Shared Auto: Bangalore's Moving Confession Booth

"Shared auto, shared auto! Koramangala, Ejipura, Sony World!" The auto driver's call rang out over the bustle of the Indiranagar metro station exit. Unlike the private auto-rickshaws I had taken in Chennai, Bangalore had perfected the art of the shared auto—vehicles that followed fixed routes, picking up and dropping off multiple passengers along the way for a fraction of the private hire cost.

I hailed one headed toward Koramangala, an area known for its concentration of tech startups and co-working spaces. The driver, a middle-aged man with salt-and-pepper hair and a face mapped with sun lines, gestured for me to get in. The small three-wheeled vehicle already held three passengers—a young woman in professional attire tapping rapidly on her phone, an elderly gentleman clutching a cloth shopping bag, and a young man whose intense phone conversation I could hear before I even settled in.

Getting into a shared auto requires a certain physical dexterity and social flexibility. The space is designed for three passengers at most, but routinely accommodates four or even five, requiring careful arrangement of limbs and belongings. I squeezed in beside the young man, our shoulders inevitably pressed together despite our mutual attempts to create space where none existed.

The auto lurched forward, its small engine straining under the weight of a full load. The open sides allowed the relatively cool Bangalore air to flow through, carrying with it the sounds and smells of the city, the honking of vehicles, the calls of street vendors, the aroma of street food, the exhaust fumes from buses and cars.

In this cramped shared space, an interesting social phenomenon occurred. Unlike in private transport where silence often reigns, the forced intimacy of the shared auto created a strange bubble where conversations happened with surprising openness. Perhaps it was the temporary nature of the journey or the unlikelihood of ever seeing fellow passengers again, but people often spoke with remarkable candor.

The Reluctant Entrepreneur

The young man beside me was deep in what appeared to be a stressful phone conversation. Dressed in a plain blue t-shirt and jeans, with tired eyes and three days' worth of stubble, he looked like many of the startup founders I had glimpsed through the windows of Bangalore's countless coffee shops.

"Maa, nanage time kodi! Success Bandre Ella Sari Aagatte!" he said in Kannada, his voice reflecting a mixture of frustration and pleading. Noticing my curious glance, he switched to English for his next sentence: "I just need some more time. The investors believe in us; why can't you?"

He ended the call with a heavy sigh, staring at his phone for a moment before slipping it into his pocket.

"Startup problems?" I ventured, making an educated guess based on his side of the conversation.

He looked at me with surprise, then smiled ruefully. "That obvious, huh?"

His name was Naveen, and he had been working on a logistics startup for the past two years. The company aimed to solve the last-mile delivery problem for small businesses in Tier 2 and Tier 3 cities—places that were underserved by the big e-commerce players.

"We just closed our second round of funding," he said, a hint of pride breaking through his exhaustion. "Two million dollars. Not huge by Bangalore standards, but enough to scale our operations to five more cities."

"Congratulations," I said. "That sounds like good news. So why the tense phone call?"

His expression darkened slightly. "That was my mother. My family thinks I'm wasting my life. I left a perfectly good job at Infosys to start this company. They still don't understand why."

Naveen had been working as a software engineer for three years before the entrepreneurial bug bit him. His family—middle-class, traditional, risk-averse—had celebrated when he landed his prestigious IT job. It represented security, respectability, and a comfortable life. His decision to leave it all behind for the uncertain world of startups had created an ongoing tension.

"Funding mil raha hai, par gharwale samajhte nahi" ~ "I'm getting funding, but my family doesn't understand," he sighed. "My father keeps saying, *'Naukri hi safe hai. Startups*

toh sirf ameer logon ka khel hai.' ~ 'Only jobs are safe. Startups are just games for rich people.'"

His father, a retired government employee, couldn't comprehend why anyone would leave a stable job for an uncertain dream. In his worldview, shaped by decades of experience in pre-liberalization India, job security was the ultimate goal. Entrepreneurship was for those who could afford to fail—people with family wealth or foreign connections to fall back on.

"The thing is," Naveen continued, "he's not entirely wrong. Nine out of ten startups fail. I've seen friends lose everything—their savings, relationships, even their health. Sometimes I wonder if I'm being foolish too."

Yet despite these doubts, Naveen's passion for his venture was palpable. His eyes lit up as he described how his platform was helping small shopkeepers compete with e-commerce giants, how it was creating employment opportunities in smaller cities, how it might eventually help bridge the digital divide that threatened to leave much of India behind.

"Lekin sir, ek chance toh lena padega, nahi?" ~ "But sir, you have to take a chance, right?" he asked, as the auto slowed for his stop near a co-working space in Koramangala.

As he paid the driver and prepared to alight, I asked if his family would come around if his startup succeeded.

He smiled. "Success has many fathers; failure is an orphan. If we make it big, they'll tell everyone it was their idea all along."

With that, he disappeared into a nondescript building that probably housed dozens of other dreamers just like him—young men and women caught between India's traditional values of security and stability and the new ethos of disruption and risk-taking that defined Bangalore's startup ecosystem.

The Security Guard Who Became His Own Boss

Later that day, I booked a cab to visit the famous Lalbagh Botanical Gardens. The driver who arrived, Shankar, was a man in his late 40s, dressed in a faded but immaculately clean shirt, with a thick mustache that seemed to be a point of pride.

"Sir, aap Bangalore naye aaye lagte ho" ~ "Sir, you seem new to Bangalore," he said, adjusting his rearview mirror after I settled in.

"Naya nahi, par alag tareeke se dekh raha hoon." ~ "Not new, but I'm seeing it differently this time."

Curious about his story, I asked how long he had been driving a cab.

"Main pehle IT company mein security guard tha, sir. Lekin lockdown ke baad naukri chali gayi. Isliye cab chalata hoon." ~ "I was a security guard at an IT company before the lockdown. But I lost my job, so now I drive a cab."

Shankar's story unfolded gradually during our journey. He had worked for eight years as a security guard at one of Bangalore's many tech parks, watching thousands of software engineers and executives pass through the gates each day. When the pandemic forced companies to implement work-from-home policies, the need for physical security diminished. Shankar, along with dozens of others, found himself unemployed at an age when new opportunities were hard to come by.

"Bangalore badal gaya hai, sir. Pichle 10 saal mein maang badh gayi, par zindagi aur mehengi ho gayi." ~ "Bangalore has

changed. In the last 10 years, demand has increased, but life has become more expensive."

With two school-going children and a wife who ran a small tiffin service from their home in the city's outskirts, Shankar needed to find income quickly. Using his savings, he obtained a car through a rental scheme connected to a ride-sharing platform.

What struck me about Shankar was his dignity and the quiet pride he took in his new profession. His car was spotless, his demeanor professional, and despite the circumstances that had forced this career change, he spoke without bitterness.

I asked if he wanted to return to his security job if the opportunity arose.

He thought for a moment before responding. "Naukri toh mil sakti hai, par yeh bhi ek tareeka hai jeene ka. Kam se kam apna malik toh main khud hoon." (I could find another job, but this is also a way to live. At least here, I'm my own boss.)

This sentiment—valuing autonomy over security—seemed to reflect a shifting mindset in Bangalore. Even for someone like Shankar, who hadn't chosen entrepreneurship so much as had it thrust upon him by circumstance, the idea of being his own boss held significant appeal.

"Earlier, I watched others come and go," he explained. "Now I have decided when I will work, how much I will work. If my son has a school function, I can attend. If business is good one day, I can take the next day off."

This newfound flexibility had changed his relationship with his family as well. "Now I understand my wife's business better," he said with pride. "Sometimes I even help her deliver tiffins to her customers when I'm not driving. We have become partners."

As we arrived at Lalbagh, I realized that Shankar, despite his modest circumstances, embodied the same entrepreneurial spirit as the well-funded startup founders in Koramangala's co-working spaces. The difference was not in the mindset but in the scale and recognition of their respective ventures.

The Engineer Who Chose Tea Over Technology

Near Jayanagar, a predominantly residential area with a more traditional feel than Koramangala's startup hub, I came across a small tea stall with an intriguing signboard: "MBA Chaiwala — Harvard Nahin, Hard Work Se Sikha Hai" (Not from Harvard, Learned from Hard Work).

The stall itself was a cut above the typical roadside tea vendor—a neat, well-designed kiosk with a small counter where customers could sit on high stools. The menu, written on a blackboard in colorful chalk, offered not just standard chai but various specialty teas and coffee, including an intriguing "Startup Special" and "Investor Pitch Pack" (a thermos of tea with disposable cups, presumably for meetings).

The owner, Karthik, looked like any other tea vendor at first glance—except for the sharp intelligence in his eyes and the careful articulation of his speech. He greeted me with a warm smile and asked, *"Saar, filter coffee try karenge?"* ~ "Sir, would you like to try filter coffee?"

As I sipped the excellent coffee, I asked about the unusual name of his shop.

"Saar, mere liye MBA ka matlab hai—Mindset, Business, and Adjustment." ~ "For me, MBA means Mindset, Business, and Adjustment."

Karthik's story was as surprising as his signboard. He had a B.Tech degree in Mechanical Engineering from a reputable college and worked for three years at a major IT service company. His corporate job had provided comfort, security, and social status—everything that traditional Indian success metrics valued.

"Corporate duniya mein kaam kiya. Phir samjha, main apna boss banna chahta hoon." ~ "I worked in the corporate world. Then I realized, I want to be my own boss."

The catalyst for this realization came during a particularly grueling project that required him to work 14-hour days implementing someone else's vision. "I was good at my job," he said, "but I kept asking myself: Am I building my future or someone else's empire?"

With the savings from his corporate stint, Karthik started his tea stall—not as a last resort but as a deliberate choice. He had analyzed the market, identified a location with high foot traffic near colleges and offices, and created a brand identity that cleverly played on his educational background.

"People laughed at first," he admitted. "My parents were heartbroken. 'We educated you for this?' they asked. My girlfriend left me. But I saw something they didn't—opportunity in the ordinary."

Two years later, his business was thriving. He had expanded from a simple cart to the current kiosk and was planning to open two more locations. His "Startup Special"—a strong masala chai designed to fuel late-night coding sessions—had developed something of a cult following among local entrepreneurs.

"Engineering sikha, par zindagi yahan sikhi." ~ "I learned engineering, but I learned life here."

What fascinated me about Karthik was how he had applied his education to a traditional business, bringing analytical thinking and innovation to something as commonplace as a tea stall. He showed me his inventory management system—a simple app he had designed himself. He explained how he had analyzed sales data to optimize his menu and hours of operation. He had even started a loyalty program using a basic digital punch card system.

"The corporate world taught me processes and analysis," he explained. "The tea stall taught me people and adaptation. Both are valuable."

As we talked, a steady stream of customers came and went—college students grabbing tea between classes, office workers on breaks, elderly neighborhood residents who clearly came as much for conversation as for beverages. Karthik greeted many by name, remembering their usual orders and asking about their lives with genuine interest.

His tea stall wasn't just a business; it was a community hub—a "third place" that wasn't home or work but somewhere people could connect, converse, and feel welcome. In creating this space, Karthik had achieved something that many well-funded startups with their ping-pong tables and beanbag chairs aspired to but rarely accomplished.

The Office Boy Who Became an Investor

My final significant encounter in Bangalore took place at a co-working space in Koramangala, where I had arranged to meet a former colleague now working with a tech startup. While waiting in the common area, I noticed a young man serving tea and coffee to various groups of earnest-looking entrepreneurs engaged in animated discussions about funding rounds, user acquisition costs, and scaling strategies.

Unlike the typical office helpers I had encountered in corporate settings, this young man seemed unusually attentive to the conversations happening around him. As he moved from table to table, I noticed how he would linger slightly, absorbing the discussions before moving on to the next group.

During a lull in the busy space, he approached me with a tray. "Tea or coffee, sir?" he asked in accented but clear English.

"Tea, please," I replied. "You seem very interested in what people are talking about here."

His eyes widened slightly, surprised at being noticed. Then he smiled. "Learning, sir. Every day, learning."

His name was Rahul, and he had been working as an office assistant at the co-working space for nearly three years. Originally from a small town in Karnataka, he had come to Bangalore with minimal education but a burning desire to improve his circumstances.

"Pehle toh sirf sunta tha. Phir socha, main bhi seekh sakta hoon." ~ “At first, I just listened. Then I thought, why can't I learn too?”

What Rahul had been doing, I discovered, was conducting an informal education in entrepreneurship and investment by carefully observing the startup founders and investors who frequented the space. He had picked up the vocabulary of venture capital, understood the basics of business models, and grasped concepts like runway, burn rate, and minimum viable product—all without any formal training.

More impressively, he had begun to apply this knowledge. Using a small portion of his modest salary, he had started investing in stocks based on insights gleaned from overhearing discussions about market trends and emerging technologies.

"First investment was 500 rupees only, sir," he told me proudly. "Now I have a portfolio of 50,000 rupees."

Rahul showed me his investment app on a basic smartphone, revealing a surprisingly sophisticated approach to building a diversified portfolio. He had investments in established blue-chip companies, a few carefully selected startups that had gone public, and even a small amount in a mutual fund focused on technology.

"Aaj bhi chai pilata hoon, par ab startup founders mujhe 'bhai' bulaate hain." ~ "I still serve tea, but now startup founders call me 'brother.'"

Some of the founders had noticed Rahul's interest and intelligence and had begun to include him in conversations, explaining concepts, answering his questions, and occasionally even asking for his perspective as someone who understood the challenges of the average Indian consumer.

Rahul's journey was perhaps the most powerful embodiment of what made Bangalore unique. In a different city, he might have remained invisible, just another service worker in the background. But in Bangalore's relatively meritocratic ecosystem, where ideas and intelligence could sometimes transcend social barriers, he had found a path to growth that didn't require formal credentials.

"My goal is not to become rich," he told me with surprising clarity. "My goal is to understand how money works. Once you understand that, you are free."

The City of Second Chances

As my time in Bangalore drew to a close, I found myself reflecting on the stories I had encountered—Naveen's struggle to pursue his startup dream despite family pressure, Shankar's reinvention as a self-employed cab driver after losing his security job, Karthik's deliberate choice to leave the corporate world for entrepreneurship, and Rahul's remarkable self-education through observation and initiative.

Each story represented a different facet of Bangalore's unique character as a city of reinvention and second chances. Unlike Mumbai, which demanded relentless hustle, or Delhi, which respected established hierarchies, or Chennai, which valued traditional knowledge, Bangalore seemed to offer space for people to rewrite their stories.

This wasn't to say that success was guaranteed or that the city didn't have deep inequalities and struggles. For every successful startup founder or engineer-turned-entrepreneur, there were countless others whose dreams had failed to materialize. The gleaming tech parks and trendy brewpubs existed alongside growing slums and communities displaced by rapid development.

But what made Bangalore different was its culture of possibility—an openness to new ideas, new identities, and new beginnings that permeated the city's atmosphere as distinctly as the scent of its flowering trees.

On my last evening, I visited Cubbon Park, a 300-acre green space in the heart of the city that offered a respite from urban intensity. As I walked its paths in the golden light of sunset, I observed the diverse cross-section of Bangalore life around me—tech workers decompressing after long hours at their screens, young couples finding privacy in a crowded city, families enjoying picnics, elderly people taking measured constitutional walks, and joggers pushing themselves along the trails.

In this momentary pause from the city's relentless forward momentum, I thought about what defined true success. Was it the exit value of a startup? The security of a government job? The freedom of self-employment? The growth of an investment portfolio?

The stories I had encountered in Bangalore suggested a different metric altogether—one based not on where you started or even where you ended up, but on how far you were willing to go in pursuit of your own definition of a meaningful life.

Naveen might never achieve the unicorn status he dreamed of, but his willingness to risk security for passion was its own form of success. Shankar hadn't chosen to become a cab driver, but his ability to find dignity and autonomy in his circumstances represented a profound achievement. Karthik had walked away from the prestige of his engineering career, but in doing so had created something uniquely his own. Rahul might never become a wealthy investor, but his determination to learn and grow despite limitations was perhaps the most inspiring success of all.

As I prepared to leave for my final destination, I carried with me a new understanding of wealth and poverty that transcended monetary measures. True poverty, I was beginning to understand, wasn't just a lack of financial resources but a lack of agency—the inability to shape one's own story. And true wealth wasn't measured in assets but in possibilities—the freedom to reimagine oneself and the courage to pursue that vision.

Bangalore, for all its contradictions and challenges, excelled at nurturing this most precious form of wealth—not promising success, but offering the far more valuable gift of possibility.

Chapter 6:
The Bus Stops: Waiting for Life's Lessons

Pauses in a Rushing World

If there is one place that forces people to pause in their fast-moving lives, it is a bus stop.

Unlike airports or railway stations—where travel is grand and planned, where announcements boom over speakers, where destinations are exotic and exciting—bus stops are humble waypoints. They are unassuming corners of daily existence where people must simply wait, often with no indicator of when their transport will arrive, no comfortable lounge to sit in, and no overpriced coffee to sip.

In the months that I spent relying on public transport across India's cities, I found myself spending countless hours at these waiting places. At first, I saw this waiting as wasted time—moments stolen from my day that could have been spent more productively. But gradually, I began to understand that these forced pauses held their own value. They were opportunities to observe, to connect, and sometimes, to glimpse profound truths about life itself.

While airports serve those who can afford to fly and train stations connect major destinations, bus stops serve everyone. They are the great democratic spaces of transportation—used by laborers and office workers, students and retirees, the privileged and the struggling. In these shared spaces of anticipation, stories unfold if you take the time to notice them.

This chapter is about those moments of waiting—about the bus stops I visited across India and the people I met there who, knowingly or unknowingly, taught me some of the most important lessons of my journey.

The Woman Who Waited Too Long

My deepening appreciation for bus stops began at Bangalore's Majestic Bus Stand—officially known as Kempegowda Bus Station, though few locals use this formal name. It is one of India's largest bus terminals, a sprawling, chaotic hub where thousands of buses depart daily for destinations across Karnataka and neighboring states.

I arrived there on a Saturday afternoon, planning to take a day trip to Mysore. The station was a symphony of sounds and movements—conductors shouting destinations, hawkers selling everything from snacks to smartphone chargers, the growl of diesel engines, the hiss of air brakes, and the constant tide of humanity flowing through the terminal's many platforms.

The air hung heavy with diesel fumes, punctuated by the aroma of fresh vada pav and the occasional waft of jasmine from a flower seller's basket. Electronic displays flickered with arrival and departure times, though most people seemed to rely on shouted information or the knowledge of regular commuters rather than these official notices.

As I waited for my bus, I noticed a young woman sitting on a bench nearby. She stood out not because of any dramatic feature but because of the stillness she maintained amid the swirling activity around her. Dressed in business casual attire—a simple kurta over jeans—she stared at the phone in her hands, her fingers hovering over the screen as if she wanted to type something but couldn't quite commit to the action.

There was a hesitancy in her movements that caught my attention— a tension between action and inaction that seemed out of place in this environment of purposeful coming and going. Occasionally, she would look up at the electronic display, then back at her phone, then out at the buses, her expression shifting between contemplation and what looked like regret.

When my bus to Mysore was delayed by 30 minutes, I decided to sit on the same bench, leaving a respectful distance between us. After a few minutes, she glanced over, and I offered a polite smile.

"Waiting long?" I asked, the universal conversation starter of bus stops worldwide.

"Too long," she replied with a sigh that seemed to carry more weight than just the frustration of a delayed bus.

Her name was Priya, and she was a software engineer working for one of Bangalore's many IT companies. Our conversation began with typical small talk but soon shifted to something deeper when I asked if she was traveling somewhere special.

"Actually, I'm not going anywhere," she admitted, gesturing with her phone. "I'm just sitting here, trying to make a decision."

She explained that she had received a job offer from a tech company in Singapore—a significant career opportunity with better pay, international exposure, and prospects for growth far beyond what was available in her current position. The deadline for accepting the offer was today.

"I've been thinking about it for weeks, but I can't seem to decide," she said, frustration evident in her voice. "My parents are against it. They worry about me being alone in a foreign country. My boyfriend wants me to stay. And part of me is scared to leave everything familiar behind."

"So, you came to a bus station to think about it?" I asked curious about her choice of location.

She smiled wryly. "I thought seeing all these people going places might give me the courage to make a move myself. But I've been sitting here for hours, and I'm still scared."

As we talked, it became clear that this wasn't just about a job offer. It was about the larger theme of opportunities and the courage required to seize them. Priya had always been the "good girl" who followed the expected path—good grades, respected engineering college, stable job, relationship heading toward marriage. The Singapore offers represented the first major deviation from that prescribed journey.

"I did the same thing last year with another opportunity," she confessed. "I hesitated, asked for more time to decide, and by the time I was ready to say yes, they had hired someone else."

Her words struck me deeply. "You should have boarded that bus when it came," I said.

She nodded. "Too late now." Looking at her phone, she added, "And maybe too late for this one too."

When I asked if she thought another opportunity would come, she smiled sadly. "Maybe. But what if I hesitate again?"

In Priya's story, I saw something universal—the tendency to wait at life's metaphorical bus stops, watching opportunities arrive and depart while we remain frozen by indecision, fear, or the weight of others' expectations. Sometimes we wait too long, and the moment passes. The bus leaves without us, and we're left wondering about the journey we might have taken.

As my bus to Mysore finally arrived, I wished her luck with her decision. Whether she accepted the Singapore offer or not, I hoped she would learn from this moment of reflection at Majestic Bus Stand—that sometimes, the greater risk is in not taking one at all.

The Man Who Was Ready to Leave

Weeks later, in Chennai, I found myself at a bus stop near T. Nagar during the golden hour of early evening. Unlike Bangalore's Majestic, this was a simpler affair—a metal shelter along a busy road, offering minimal protection from the elements but serving as a vital connection point for the area's residents.

The atmosphere here was different—less frantic than Majestic, with a steady but manageable flow of people coming and going. The setting sun cast long shadows and bathed everything in a warm, golden light that softened the hard edges of urban life. The air carried the scent of jasmine from a nearby temple and the spicy aroma of roasting peanuts from a vendor's cart.

Among those waiting was an elderly man who immediately caught my eye. In a sea of casual attire and working clothes, he stood out in his crisp white dhoti and shirt, immaculately pressed despite the heat and humidity. His silver hair was neatly combed, and a simple cloth bag rested on his lap. Unlike the restless energy of most waiting passengers, he emanated a remarkable calm, sitting with perfect posture and an expression of serene acceptance.

As the minutes passed and buses came and went, I noticed that he made no move to board any of them, despite checking each one carefully as it arrived. Curious, I took a seat beside him and nodded in greeting.

"You seem very patient," I remarked. "Waiting for a specific bus?"

He turned to me with a gentle smile that crinkled the corners of his eyes. "I am not sure. But I know I won't be coming back."

His unexpected response intrigued me, and as we fell into conversation, he shared his story. His name was Venkatesh, and he had lived in Chennai for fifty years, working as a schoolteacher until his retirement a decade ago. Now widowed, with his children settled in America, he had made the decision to return to his ancestral village in Tamil Nadu's interior.

"I lived in this city for 50 years. Worked hard, raised a family. But now, my wife is gone, and my children have their own lives abroad. This house, these streets... they don't feel like mine anymore. So, I am going back to my village. To the place where I was born."

When I asked if he was sad to leave the city where he had spent most of his life, he shook his head.

"Not sad, son. Just... accepting. Life is like a bus journey. You get on, you enjoy the ride, and then, when it's time, you get off at your stop."

There was something profound in the simplicity of his words. Unlike Priya in Bangalore, who struggled with the decision to board her metaphorical bus to Singapore, Venkatesh had made peace with the natural conclusion of his urban journey. He wasn't clinging to the familiar or fearing the unknown—he was simply recognizing when one chapter ended and another began.

"Will your children visit you in the village?" I asked.

"Perhaps. But they belong to a different world now. America has become their home. And soon, my village will be mine again." He patted his cloth bag. "I don't need much. Just my clothes, some photographs, and my memories."

As the sun dipped lower and the street lights began to flicker on, Venkatesh stood up as a bus approached. "This is my bus," he said with quiet certainty.

"How do you know?" I asked, not having heard any announcement.

He smiled. "When you're ready to leave, the right bus always comes."

I watched him board with dignified steps, finding a window seat where he raised his hand in a small farewell gesture as the bus pulled away. I never learned which village he was heading to or what awaited him there. But his lesson stayed with me—that letting go is not always a loss. Sometimes, it is simply life guiding us to where we need to be next.

The Father Who Couldn't Rest

The bus stand near AIIMS in Delhi presented yet another face of India's waiting spaces. Located near one of the country's premier medical institutions, this stop served a unique mix of people—medical professionals in white coats, anxious families of patients, students from the nearby universities, and regular commuters navigating Delhi's sprawling landscape.

The atmosphere here carried a palpable tension absent from other bus stops. For many waiting here, the journey wasn't about commuting to work or visiting family—it was part of a desperate search for healing, for answers, for hope in the face of illness. The proximity to the hospital gave this ordinary bus stop an extraordinary context, where everyday concerns seemed trivial compared to the life-and-death matters being faced just across the street.

It was a crisp winter evening, with Delhi's infamous pollution creating a hazy glow around the streetlights, when I noticed a man in his thirties sitting on a bench with a young girl, perhaps six or seven years old. What caught my attention was the contrast between them—the man looked utterly exhausted, with dark circles under his eyes and shoulders slumped from what seemed like the weight of the world, while the little girl was animated and bright, playing some sort of hand game to entertain herself.

The father (as I assumed he was) had the weathered look of someone who hadn't slept properly in days. His clothes were wrinkled but clean, suggesting care despite difficult circumstances. Every few minutes, he would check his watch, then scan the road for approaching buses, then look back at his daughter with a smile that transformed his tired face momentarily.

The girl, oblivious to whatever burdens her father carried, had turned their waiting time into an opportunity for play. She was drawing patterns on the fogged-up glass of the bus shelter, counting passing cars of different colors, and occasionally tugging at her father's sleeve to show him something interesting she had noticed.

"Aap tension mat lo, main madad karta hoon" ~ "Don't worry, I'll help," I heard him say to her at one point, his voice gentle despite his obvious fatigue.

When the girl wandered a few steps away to examine a street vendor's balloons, I caught the father's eye and offered a smile of acknowledgement—the universal signal of parents everywhere that says, "Kids, right?"

He returned the smile, and that small moment of connection led to conversation. His name was Ravi, and as I had guessed, he was raising his daughter alone after losing his wife to cancer two years earlier. He worked two jobs—as a hospital cleaner in the mornings and a delivery worker in the evenings—while trying to maintain some semblance of normalcy for his daughter.

"Meri beti ke liye ek behtar zindagi chahiye, sir. Main thak sakta hoon, par ruk nahi sakta." ~ "I want a better life for my daughter, sir. I may get tired, but I cannot stop."

"Today," he explained, "it was unusual." His daughter's school had closed early due to a water supply issue, disrupting his carefully orchestrated schedule. He had picked her up during his brief break between jobs and was now taking her to a neighbor who would watch her until he finished his evening shift.

"Sometimes I feel like I'm always running, always waiting, never arriving," he said, checking his watch again. "But what choice do I have?"

Despite the exhaustion evident in every line of his face, there was not a trace of self-pity in his words—only determination. He had responsibilities, and he would meet them, regardless of the personal cost.

When his bus finally arrived, he efficiently gathered their belongings and took his daughter's hand. "*Chalo, beta.* Time to go."

She looked up at him with complete trust and took his hand. As they boarded, I noticed how he positioned himself to shield her from the push of the crowd, his body becoming a protective barrier between his child and the world's rougher edges.

Watching them disappear into the bus, I was struck by a profound realization: Some people wait for life to get easier, for circumstances to improve, for the "right" bus to come along. Others, like Ravi, simply move forward, navigating whatever vehicles life provides, carrying their precious cargo with quiet dignity.

The Boy Who Found Joy in Little Things

My final bus stop lesson came from an unexpected teacher at Mumbai's Dadar Station—one of the city's busiest transit hubs where suburban trains and buses converge in a perpetual storm of human movement.

The evening rush hour was in full swing, with office workers streaming from the train station to the bus stops in an endless river of humanity. The tempo here was different from other cities—faster, more urgent, with Mumbai's characteristic no-nonsense efficiency driving every movement. Vendors called out their wares, competing with the noise of traffic and the general hum of thousands of conversations happening simultaneously.

Among this sea of purposeful adults, I noticed a young boy, no older than ten, selling colorful balloons. His clothes were torn and dusty, his small body thin but wiry with the resilience of street children everywhere. What made him stand out in the crowd wasn't his appearance but the extraordinary brightness of his smile and the luminous quality of his eyes—as if he possessed some secret joy unknown to the harried adults rushing past him.

While other vendors aggressively pursued potential customers, this boy had a different approach. He simply held his balloons high, let their colors catch the evening light, and smiled. Somehow, his quiet presence was more effective than shouting would have been. I watched as several people, perhaps touched by that smile or momentarily reconnecting with their own childhood, stopped to purchase his wares.

When the initial rush subsided, I approached him and bought a balloon—a simple red one that reminded me of a childhood I had almost forgotten.

"Bhaiyya, yeh road hi toh school hai!" ~ "Brother, this street itself is my school!" he replied with a grin when I asked if he attended school.

He told me he lived under a nearby flyover with his mother, who worked as a maid in several homes. He sold balloons while she worked, and they pooled their earnings for rent, food, and—I was surprised to learn—his schoolbooks. Despite not attending formal classes, he was teaching himself to read with secondhand textbooks purchased from a street vendor.

"Par bhaiyya, ek baat bataun?" ~ "But brother, can I tell you something?" he said excitedly, lowering his voice conspiratorially.

"Aaj mummy ne mere liye ek chocolate laya tha! Sabse badhiya din tha!" ~ "Today, my mom brought me chocolate! It was the best day ever!"

The pure, unrestrained joy in his voice as he spoke about this small luxury— a chocolate that would be an afterthought for most people—was both heart-wrenching and deeply instructive.

Here was a boy who had almost nothing by conventional standards— no proper home, no formal education, no security beyond what each day's labor could provide. Yet he had found a way to experience joy in the smallest pleasures, to maintain hope despite circumstances that would crush many adults.

His happiness came not from what he lacked, but from what little he had—a mother who loved him enough to bring him chocolate, balloons that made people smile, and the freedom to teach himself at his own pace.

"Kya tum kabhi udaas hote ho?" ~ "Do you ever feel sad?" I asked, curious about his seemingly unshakeable optimism.

He thought for a moment, his young face suddenly serious. *"Kabhi kabhi. Par udaas rehne se balloon bhi nahi bikte."* ~ "Sometimes. But staying sad doesn't sell balloons either."

There was wisdom in his pragmatism—a reminder that gratitude is not about how much we have but about how we choose to see what we have. It's a perspective that can turn a simple chocolate into a cause for celebration or transform a hard day of selling balloons into an opportunity for learning.

As I watched him approach another potential customer, balloon strings held high and a smile firmly in place, I wondered how many of us had forgotten this essential truth—that joy is not a product of circumstance but a choice we make regardless of it.

Life's Different Waiting Periods

As my journey across India neared its conclusion, I found myself at one final bus stop—this one in South Mumbai, waiting for transportation back to my temporary lodging. As I sat there, watching the familiar rhythm of arrivals and departures, I reflected on all I had witnessed at these humble waypoints.

Each bus stop had revealed a different lesson about waiting and journey:

Priya at Bangalore's Majestic had shown me how we sometimes wait too long, watching opportunities pass by until it's too late to board.

Venkatesh at Chennai's T. Nagar had demonstrated the grace of knowing when it's time to leave, understanding that endings are as natural as beginnings.

Ravi at Delhi's AIIMS stop had exemplified how some journeys offer no rest—only the determination to keep going for the sake of those who depend on us.

And the balloon seller at Dadar had taught me that no matter where the journey takes us, joy can be found in the smallest moments if we choose to see them.

We all wait at different bus stops in life—for love, success, peace, or a second chance. Some wait too long. Some leave too soon. Some step onto the wrong bus and must find their way back. But in the end, every journey teaches us something, whether or not it takes us where we intended to go.

As a bus approached and I prepared to board, I thought about my own journey—from the air-conditioned comfort of my Mercedes to the crowded democracy of public transportation. I had started by selling a car at a financial loss, but what I had gained in return was beyond price—a collection of human stories that had expanded my understanding of life itself.

The simple act of waiting—something I would have once considered a waste of valuable time—had become an opportunity for connection, reflection, and growth. Perhaps that was the final lesson of the bus stops: that the pauses between destinations are not empty spaces to be endured but fertile ground where wisdom takes root.

And with that thought, I boarded my final bus, no longer just a passive passenger but an active participant in the journey itself.

Chapter 7:
Street Food and Soul Food

More Than Just a Meal

The street food of India has a certain charm.

It's about more than just hunger. It's about more than just flavor. This is about tales that come on a platter.

Stories of hardship, hope, and perseverance abound at every roadside booth, pushcart, and improvised shelter beneath a worn umbrella.

I used to eat street food every once in a while, before I sold my Mercedes just for the "experience," to bring up at dinner parties. "Oh, you must try the vada pav outside Dadar station," I would playfully tell my similarly fortunate pals, as if imparting exclusive wisdom.

Looking back, I realize how naive I was.

As I traveled across India, I came to understand that street sellers are more than simply chefs; they are also historians, philosophers, and storytellers. Their hands are skilled storytellers as much as they are cooks. Their stalls are more than just places to sell chutney and masala; they are stages upon which deep life lessons are given.

Even while Indian street cuisine is absolutely delicious, that is not the focus of this chapter. This is about the lives of the individuals who work the counters and ladles, as well as the knowledge that is offered freely with each plate.

The Scientist Who Sells Vada Pav — Mumbai

Near Mumbai's Churchgate station, it was bustling on a weekday morning. The area was alive with the sound of horns and hawkers that characterize Mumbai, as well as office-goers hurrying to work and college students lingering with backpacks.

A vada pav stand with a tiny throng beckoned to me, so I pulled over. The vendor, a middle-aged man with salt-and-pepper hair and spectacles that continually slid down his nose, walked with precision as if on a clock. He could hardly keep his hands on the pav, chutney, golden-fried potato vada, garlic, chili powder, and newspaper as he skillfully arranged all the ingredients.

Years of practice were evident in the efficiency of his motions. Every moment counted;, every action had a purpose.

Prakash was well-known in the region for his vada pav. The crisp coating, the soft pav, and the delicately spiced potato filling created a symphony of tastes that halted even the most harried office worker in their tracks.

Taking delight in the mundane act of observing a master at work, I lingered at his stall as the morning rush subsided.

"*Bhaiyya, aap kab se yeh kaam kar rahe ho?*" ~ "Brother, how long have you been doing this work?" I asked.

He looked up, his eyes meeting mine briefly before returning to his work. "*Pandrah saal.*" ~ "Fifteen years."

There was something about his brief answer, the precise way he spoke, that made me curious. Most street vendors I'd met were chatty, eager to build rapport with customers. Prakash seemed different— more reserved, more... precise.

"*Aapne pehle kuch aur kiya tha?*" ~ "Did you do something else before this?"

He hesitated, and then something shifted in his posture. He straightened up slightly, and when he spoke again, his entire manner had changed.

"*Yes, I was a research scientist with a Ph.D. in Organic Chemistry from IIT Bombay.*"

The perfect English, the technical terminology, the sudden confidence in his voice—I almost dropped my vada pav in surprise.

"*You're joking, right?*" I blurted out.

He smiled, but there was no humor in it. "*No, sir. I spent twelve years in a private laboratory working on polymer research. Then the company shut down during an economic downturn, and at forty-five, no one wanted to hire a specialized researcher whose papers were all under company patents.*"

As he spoke, his hands never stopped working—cutting more pav, preparing for the next rush. But his speech had transformed completely. Gone was the street vendor's economical Mumbai Hindi, replaced by the articulate English of an academic.

"*I applied to seventy-eight positions in six months. Got seven interviews, zero offers. Always the same feedback—overqualified, would demand too much salary, wouldn't adjust to a new team.*"

"*What made you choose this?*" I asked, gesturing to his stall.

"*Necessity, at first. My daughter was in college, my son was in high school. My wife was already working two jobs. Something I had to give.*" He paused, flipping a batch of vadas in hot oil. "*But later... there was a certain peace in this. No office politics, no arbitrary deadlines, no pretending my research mattered when the company could shut it down on a whim.*"

A group of college students approached, and his demeanor shifted once more— back to the efficient street vendor, serving vada pavs with swift movements and minimal words.

When they left, I asked him, "*Don't you ever feel that your education, and your talent are being wasted?*"

He looked at me with surprising intensity. "*Sahib, meri izzat chhoti nahi hui hai. Sirf mera kaam badal gaya hai.*" (Sir, my respect hasn't diminished. Only my work has changed.)

Then, in perfect English again: "*Einstein said, 'If you judge a fish by its ability to climb a tree, it will live its whole life believing it is stupid.' Society judged me by my ability to fit into a system that had no place for me. I chose to swim in different waters.*"

As I walked out the door with my second vada pav of the day, I couldn't help but reflect on the hidden stories behind the people we encounter daily. I wonder how many brilliant minds were hiding out behind roadside stands, operating autorickshaws or pulling carts—not because they were incapable, but because society had ignored them.

Prakash had figured out how to stay alive and had discovered a new form of happiness. The story he told was about more than simply eating; it was about the honor of starting over.

The Singer Who Became a Kebab Master — Delhi

As the sun sets, the winding streets of Old Delhi come to life. The streets come alive with the scent of spices, the sound of enthusiastic bargaining, and the sight of open-fire cooking as the intense heat of the day fades.

A tiny kebab stood with a throng of people beckoning to me as I passed Jama Masjid. A middle-aged man stood over a burning grill, the flickering flames beneath casting light on his face. As he expertly skewered meat over the charcoal fire, sprinkled spices with pinpoint accuracy, and judged doneness with a glance, his hands worked with hypnotic ease.

Every sense was delighted by the sight of *roomali roti* encasing nicely charred seekh kebabs, the perfume of smoke wafting into the night air, and the sizzle of fat dripping into hot coals.

"*Bhaijaan, ek plate seekh kebab*" ~ "Brother, one plate of seekh kebab," I said, squeezing into the crowd.

The man nodded without looking up, his focus unwavering. As he handed me my plate, I noticed his hands—rough and calloused yet moving with an artist's delicacy.

"*Gulzar Chacha ke kebab duniya mein sabse achhe hain*" ~ "Uncle Gulzar's kebabs are the best in the world," said a young man next to me, already halfway through his plate.

Gulzar smiled slightly at the praise but didn't speak. There was a quiet dignity about him, a certain melancholy in his eyes that contrasted with the vibrant energy of his cooking.

Later, as the crowd thinned out, I approached him again.

"*Aap kitne saalon se yeh kaam kar rahe hain?*" ~ "How many years have you been doing this work?"

He wiped his brow with a small towel. "*Bees saal ho gaye, sahab. Par pehle main gaana gata tha.*" ~ "Twenty years now, sir. But before this, I used to sing."

His voice, even in casual conversation, had a melodious quality to it.

"*Gaate the? Kahaan?*" ~ "You used to sing? Where?"

"*Shaadiyaan, mehfilen, chhote-mote function. Kabhi radio pe bhi gaaya tha.*" ~ "Weddings, gatherings, small functions. I even sang on the radio sometimes."

As he spoke, he continued to prepare kebabs, his movements never faltering. He told me how he had once been part of a small orchestra that performed at Delhi weddings. His specialty had been ghazals and old film songs. People would request their favorites, and he would sing deep into the night, his voice carrying stories of love and longing.

"*Phir kya hua?*" "Then what happened?" I asked.

He sighed, turning a skewer with particular care. "*Zamana badal gaya, sahab. DJ aa gaye, recorded music aa gayi. Shaadiyaan chhoti hone lagi, kharcha kam karne ke liye. Live singers ke liye jagah kam ho gayi.*" ~ "Times changed, sir. DJs came, and recorded music came. Weddings got smaller to cut costs. There was less room for live singers."

With a family to feed and rent to pay, Gulzar had to adapt. A cousin who owned a small eatery taught him to make kebabs, and gradually, he developed his own style, his own recipes.

"*Kabhi gaane ka mann nahi karta?*" ~ "Don't you ever feel like singing?" I asked.

He looked up from his grill, and for a moment, I saw a flash of the performer he once was.

"*Har roz karta hai, sahab. Par ab audience badal gayi hai.*" ~ "Every day, sir. But now my audience has changed." He gestured to the sizzling kebabs. "*Jab log mere kebab ke tareef karte hain, toh lagta hai jaise koi taaliyan bajaa raha hai.*" ~ "When people praise my kebabs, it feels like someone is applauding."

Gulzar quickly regained his composure as a customer shouted an order, ending his fleeting moment of exposure. I realized I was witnessing a different type of performance, though, as I watched him make yet another platter of kebabs—every motion deliberate, every spice measured by eye, and every skewer turned at the correct moment.

The artistry was still there, even though the stage and instrument had changed. Resilience, discovering new avenues of expression when old ones close, and maintaining dignity in the face of change were themes that resonated with me in Gulzar's novel.

The kebabs he served weren't mere fare. Songs he could no longer perform, but which he had written with the same fervor and offered to an audience that had lost the art of listening.

The Idli Amma of Marina Beach — Chennai

Marina Beach in Chennai has a unique feel to its morning light. As the sun rises over the Bay of Bengal, it creates a golden glow that softens the world's edges. By 6 a.m., the beach is alive with walkers, joggers, youngsters playing cricket, and vendors preparing for the day.

Among them was a small stall with a faded wooden table, a steel pot, and a few plastic stools. Behind it stood an elderly woman dressed in a worn cotton saree, her silver hair held back in a tight bun, her face a map of wrinkles from decades of sun exposure.

Everyone referred to her as *"Idli Amma"* ~ “Idli Mother”, and her idlis—soft, fluffy rice cakes served with coconut chutney—were popular among the locals.

I approached her stand, lured by the simplicity of her setup and the mass of early morning customers—laborers eating breakfast before work, fishermen returning from a night at sea, and office workers grabbing a quick snack before heading to their air-conditioned offices.

"*Rendu idli, amma*" ~ "Two idlis, mother," I said in my broken Tamil, holding up two fingers to make sure she understood.

She nodded, her actions remarkably swift and precise for her age. Her hands moved with practiced ease, placing idlis on a banana leaf and ladling chutney into a little indentation on the side.

As I ate, I marveled at the ideal texture—soft but firm, with just the right amount of tanginess. The chutney had a tinge of ginger that cut through the richness of the coconut, providing a balance that defied the dish's simplicity.

When I finished, I asked in Hindi, hoping she might understand, "*Aap kitne saalon se yahan hain?*" ~ "How many years have you been here?"

She looked at me, her eyes suddenly alert with understanding. "*Muttai varushama.*" Then, struggling with Hindi, "*Tees saal. Jab mere pati chale gaye.*" ~ "Thirty years. Since my husband passed away."

I was surprised she understood and responded in Hindi. "*Aap Hindi bolte hain?*" "You speak Hindi?"

She smiled, revealing several missing teeth. "*Thoda thoda. Customer aate hain north se. Seekh liya.*" ~ "A little. Customers come from the north. I learned."

She recounted her narrative over the following twenty minutes, using a combination of bad Hindi, English, and gestures. Her husband died abruptly after a heart attack, leaving her alone with three young children and no skills other than cooking. She had two choices: beg or work.

"*Bhookh sabse badi bimari hai, beta*" ~ "Hunger is the worst disease, son," she said, her eyes distant with memory. "*Mere bacche ko bhookh lagi thi. Main kya karti?*" ~ "My children were hungry. What could I do?"

So, she started selling idlis, making them in her small home and bringing them to the beach where customers were plentiful. For thirty years, she had been waking up at 3 AM to prepare the batter, steam the idlis, and make the chutney before arriving at her spot by 5:30 AM.

Her children were grown now—one son was a bank clerk, one daughter was a teacher, and another son worked in Singapore. They had asked her to stop working, to come live with them in comfort. But she refused.

"*Kaam mera life hai*" ~ "Work is my life," she explained, her hands continuing to serve customers even as she spoke to me. "*Aur bhookh walon ko khilana mera dharm.*" ~ "And feeding the hungry is my duty."

I noticed then what I hadn't seen before—a small pile of idlis wrapped in banana leaves at the corner of her table. When I asked about them, she pointed to a group of street children playing nearby.

"*Paisa dene wale, paisa dete hain. Bhookh waale, khana paate hain.*" ~ "Those who can pay, pay. Those who are hungry, get food."

Every day, she set aside a portion of her idlis for those who couldn't afford to pay—children, beggars, and the elderly with no family.

"*Jab tak haath hilte rahenge, idli banti rahegi*" ~ "As long as my hands move, the idlis will be made," she said, showing me her palms—calloused, burnt in places from years of steam, but still strong and capable.

As I watched her serve the next customer with the same care she'd shown for three decades, I was amazed by this tiny woman's resilience. Her stand was more than simply a business; it represented her dignity, her unwillingness to be defeated by circumstances, and her daily act of compassion in a world that had shown her nothing.

Idli Amma's story taught me that the most basic foods can carry the most profound meaning. Her idlis were more than just steamed rice cakes; they represented a mother's drive to survive, provide, and give even when she had little of her own.

The Panipuri Wala Who Tracked His Children's Homework — Kolkata

In the bustling streets of Kolkata's New Market district, surrounded by shoppers haggling over everything from saris to spices, I came across a panipuri stall that piqued my interest not for its food, but for its peculiar arrangement.

Ratan, a slender man in his forties, had a curious item on his cart: a little blackboard with nicely written math problems pinned next to his spice canisters.

As he served customers the wonderful hollow puris filled with spicy tamarind water, potato, and chickpeas, he would occasionally look at the board, as if to remind himself of something essential.

Intrigued, I ordered a plate and inquired about the whiteboard.

"*Yeh mere bacchon ka homework hai, sahab*" ~ "This is my children's homework, sir," he explained with a proud smile. "*Unko check karta hoon jab woh school se aate hain.*" ~ "I check it when they come from school."

Ratan's story unfolded between serving customers. His wife had died five years ago, leaving him to raise their three children alone. He had promised her that the children would receive a good education, no matter what.

"*Mere papa ne mujhe dasvi tak padhaya. Main mere bacchon ko graduate banaunga.*" ~ "My father educated me until tenth grade. I will make my children graduates."

His day began at 4 AM, preparing ingredients for his panipuri stall. By 7 AM, he would wake his children, help them dress for school, and pack their lunches. Then he'd wheel his cart to this busy corner where he worked until 9 PM.

"*Bacche school se seedhe yahan aate hain. Homework kar lete hain mere paas baithke, phir ghar jaate hain mere bade bhaiya ke saath.*" ~ "The children come straight here from school. They do their homework sitting with me, then go home with my elder brother."

The whiteboard, he explained, was his way of staying involved in their education despite his limited schooling. Every morning, he would write down their homework assignments and check them when the children arrived after school.

"*Mujhe maths samajh mein nahi aati, lekin main solution dekh sakta hoon. Galat hai ki sahi, pata chal jata hai.*" ~ "I don't understand math, but I can see the solution. I can tell if it's wrong or right."

As we spoke, a young girl in a school uniform approached the stand, her face beaming when she noticed Ratan. Priya, his daughter, was coming directly from school, as she always did.

After hugging her father, she sat on a small stool next to the cart and pulled out her books. Ratan served customers with one eye on her task, occasionally pausing to check her notes and inquire about their day.

The sight was both regular and extraordinary: a father assisting with schoolwork while selling street food, and a child studying amid the noise and bustle of one of Kolkata's largest markets.

When business slowed down, Ratan handed me a tiny notebook he kept under his cash box. It contained nicely written report card entries for all three children, charting their progress over the years.

"*Meri beti doctor banegi*" ~ "My daughter will become a doctor," he said, his eyes shining with conviction. "*Bada beta engineer. Chhota abhi decide nahi kiya, lekin woh bhi kuch bada karega.*" ~ "Elder son an engineer. The younger one hasn't decided yet, but he'll do something big too."

What impressed me most about Ratan was not only his commitment to his children's education, but also his straightforward attitude to it. There was no self-pity or lingering on hardships. Just a father doing what had to be done and making the best of his situation.

"*Log kehte hain main galat karta hoon—bacchon ko yahan market mein laake. Unko ghar pe study karna chahiye, tuition teacher ke saath.*" ~ "People say I'm wrong—bringing my children here to the market. They should study at home, with a tuition teacher."

He shook his head, adding more tamarind water to a customer's panipuri.

"*Par main samajhta hoon—bacchon ko life ka lesson bhi seekhna chahiye. Mehnat kya hoti hai, struggle kya hota hai. Tabhi woh life mein strong banenge.*" ~ "But I understand—children should also learn life's lessons. What hard work is, what struggle is. Only then will they become strong in life."

Watching Priya complete her homework beside her father's cart, occasionally looking up to smile at customers or assist pack panipuris in a hurry, I wondered if she wasn't receiving a far more useful education than what was taught in schools.

Ratan's panipuri booth was more than just a place to eat; it served as a classroom for his children, teaching them tenacity, dignity, and the unbreakable force of parental love.

The Chaat Seller Who Used to Be a Masterchef — Lucknow

Lucknow, the city of nawabs and kebabs, where food is more than simply a source of nourishment; it is a cultural heritage, an art form passed down through centuries.

In a corner of the famous Hazratganj market, I discovered a chaat stall unlike any other. The setup was straightforward—a wooden cart with metal canisters carrying various chutneys and toppings—but the man behind it moved with an elegance that looked out of place on a street corner.

Anwar Mian, as everyone called him, was in his sixties, with a perfectly groomed white beard and the aristocratic demeanor of someone used to commanding attention. His hands moved like a conductor's—a dash of spice here, a drip of tamarind water there, each plate of papri chaat or dahi bhalla put together with precision timing and artistic flare.

What drew my attention was not the food, but the mob that had collected around his stand. Unlike most street food sellers, Anwar's clients ranged from laborers to businesspeople in fancy suits, all of whom waited patiently for their turn.

After eating my plate of chaat—which was the right combination of crispy, sour, sweet, and spicy—I asked the businessman next to me why this particular stall was so popular.

"*Yeh sirf chaat nahi bana rahe hain, sahab. Yeh history bana rahe hain*" ~ "He's not just making chaat, sir. He's making history," he replied. "*Anwar Mian pehle Nawab ke kitchen mein head chef the. Unki family saat peediyon se royal khana banati aayi hai.*" ~ "Anwar Mian was previously the head chef in the Nawab's kitchen. His family has been cooking royal food for seven generations."

Intrigued, I waited until the evening rush eased before approaching Anwar Mian. He offered me a seat on a small stool by his cart while he prepared for the next day by slicing veggies and combining spices.

His story was like something out of a historical novel. His family had been royal cooks for the Nawabs of Awadh for generations, keeping secret recipes that were considered culinary jewels. Anwar had previously trained under his father and grandfather before becoming a master chef in one of Lucknow's most prestigious kitchens, where he prepared extravagant feasts for dignitaries and celebrities.

"*Humari zubaan pe bada bharosa tha unko,*" ~ "They trusted our palate greatly" he said, his eyes distant with memory. "*Ek baar chhuko, aur pata chal jata tha ki namak kam hai ya masala zyada.*" ~ "One taste, and we could tell if the salt was too little or the spice too much."

When I asked why he left such a prestigious position for a street cart, his expression sobered.

"*Zamaana badla, sahab. Naye maalik aaye, purane tareeke badalne lage. Machine se bana hua masala, frozen ingredients, microwave mein garam kiya hua khana.*" ~ "Times changed, sir. New owners came, old methods started changing.

Machine-made spices, frozen ingredients, food heated in a microwave."

The final straw came when he was asked to prepare a "fusion" version of a centuries-old recipe to make it more appealing to foreign tourists.

"*Mere buzurg kabr mein karwat lete*" ~ "My ancestors would turn in their graves," he said quietly. "*Humne unke haath ke neeche seekha tha ki khaane ki izzat karo. Usse sirf paisa kamane ka zariya mat banao.*" ~ "We learned under their hands to respect food. Don't make it just a means to earn money."

So Anwar Mian left the prestigious hotel kitchen and, with the savings from his decades of service, set up a humble chaat stall. His reasoning was simple: "*Chaat hamari awaam ka khana hai—simple, saccha, aur seedha. Ismein koi compromise nahi karna padta.*" ~ "Chaat is the food of our people—simple, honest, and straightforward. In this, I don't have to compromise."

Word of his extraordinary skill spread quickly. People who could never have afforded to taste his cooking in the royal kitchens could now experience his mastery for the price of a plate of chaat.

"*Ab meri kitchen chhoti hai, lekin mere customers ki sankhya badi hai*" ~ "Now my kitchen is small, but the number of my customers is large," he said with quiet pride.

As he spoke, a young chef from one of Lucknow's five-star hotels approached the stall. He greeted Anwar Mian with folded hands, touching his feet in respect.

"*Ustaad, aap se seekhne aaya hoon. Hotel mein kuch naya add karna hai menu mein.*" ~ "Master, I've come to learn from you. We need to add something new to the hotel menu."

Anwar smiled. "*Naya add karne se pehle, purana seekho, beta. Bunyaad mazboot honi chahiye.*" ~ "Before adding something new, learn the old, son. The foundation should be strong."

For the next hour, I watched as the elderly chaat vendor gently taught the professionally educated young chef how to balance flavors, how to discern spices by smell rather than quantity, and how to honor rather than disguise the ingredients.

In that moment, I realized that Anwar Mian hadn't resigned—he had elevated street food to an art form, democratizing what had previously been exclusive and safeguarding traditions that would otherwise have been lost to commerce.

His chaat stall wasn't simply about business. It was a classroom, a cultural archive, and a statement about what is actually important in food—not prestige or profit, but respect for ingredients, history, and the people you feed.

The Stories Behind Every Plate

As my journey through India progressed, I discovered countless more stories hidden behind street food stalls—the college professor who sold momos after his university closed, the former athlete who made dosas after an injury ended his career, and the refugee who brought his homeland's flavors to a new city.

Street food, I found, is never just about satisfying hungry bellies. It's about dreams, sacrifices, adaptations, and the irrepressible human spirit that finds beauty even in adversity.

Next time you stop at a roadside kiosk for a quick bite, take a peek at the hands that serve you. Those hands may have previously undertaken laboratory research, composed heartfelt music, cooked for royalty, or developed enterprises. Those hands could be helping children with their schooling, preserving historical recipes, or starting anew.

The flavor on your tongue may be great, but the story behind it could be remarkable.

Street food is not simply soul food because it satisfies a hunger. It's soul food because it contains the souls of those who make it—their histories, hopes, and unspoken determination to transform whatever life has given them into something nourishing, important, and worthy of sharing.

In the end, isn't that what we're all striving to accomplish?

Chapter 8:
The Haircut Chronicles

The Unsung Sanctuaries of Men

A barbershop provides more than simply haircuts.

It is a confession booth where men may freely express themselves, a debating platform where thoughts can flow without judgment, a social club where strangers can develop friendships, and, on occasion, a therapist's office where problems can be discussed without an appointment.

Unlike the upscale salons with their pristine interiors and hushed chats, the local roadside barbershop is where real life happens—raw, unfiltered, and authentic.

In these modest places, folks from various walks of life sit side by side—the laborer next to the lawyer, the student next to the older citizen. For a brief period, when the scissors snip and the razor glides, social barriers melt. Surrendering to another man's blade fosters a unique intimacy and vulnerability in men who are schooled to constantly appear powerful.

During my tour across India, I learned that getting a haircut may provide an incredible insight into the human condition. Each city's barbershops had their own personality, rhythm, and stories waiting to be told.

The Poet with the Scissors — Mumbai

In Mumbai's Girgaon neighborhood, tucked between a paan shop and a small shrine, I discovered a barbershop that appeared locked in time. The paint was peeling from the walls, the mirrors had clouded edges, and two old-fashioned chairs with rust patches on their metal arms confronted a counter crowded with combs, scissors, and amber bottles of hair tonic.

An antiquated radio played classic Hindi tunes by Kishore Kumar and Mohammad Rafi, periodically interrupted by static. The floor was strewn with hair clippings, which were scooped into mounds but never completely eliminated.

Iqbal Bhai, the barber, was an elderly guy with a well-trimmed white beard and steady, calm hands. Despite his age—I subsequently discovered he was nearly seventy—his motions were precise, and his eyes were sharp beneath steel-rimmed glasses. He worked in solitude, concentrating solely on his skill, with the dignity of a physician rather than a plain barber.

As I slid into the creaky chair, he put a faded cloth over my clothes and looked at me in the mirror.

"*Kya karna hai, sahab?*" ~ "What do you want done, sir?" he asked, his voice gentle but clear.

"*Bas thoda chota kar dijiye*" ~ "Just make it a little shorter," I replied.

He nodded and got to work, his fingers gliding through my hair with accustomed ease. The snip of his scissors generated a rhythm that complemented the cinematic music playing in the background. We remained silent for several minutes, he is working and me studying his reflection in the mirror.

His presence was comforting, and his serene assurance made me feel safe. This was more than simply a haircut; it was a masterful performance.

"*Aap yahan naye lagte ho*" ~ "You seem new here," he finally said, breaking the silence.

"*Haan, bas chal raha hoon, alag nazariye se sheher dekh raha hoon*" ~ "Yes, just traveling, seeing the city from a different perspective," I explained.

A small smile appeared beneath his white mustache. "*Nazariya badalne se duniya bhi badal jati hai, sahab*" ~ "When your perspective changes, so does the world," he said, his words carrying a weight that surprised me.

This wasn't the typical barber small talk I was used to.

As he continued cutting, I asked him how long he had been in this profession.

"*Pichle 40 saal se. Pehle main shayari karta tha,*" ~ "For the last 40 years. Before that, I was a poet) he replied, matter-of-factly"

I nearly turned my head in surprise, but his firm hand kept me in place.

"*Poet? Toh phir yeh kaam?*" ~ "A poet? Then why this work?" I couldn't help asking.

He laughed softly, a gentle sound that carried no bitterness.

"*Beta, paet ki bhook shayari se nahi bharti. Lekin zindagi ka har pal ek nazm ki tarah hai,*" ~ "Son, poetry doesn't fill the stomach. But every moment in life is like a poem," he said, continuing to trim my hair with the same careful attention.

As he worked, he told me his story. In his youth, Iqbal Bhai had been part of Mumbai's Urdu poetry circle, performing at mushairas and poetry gatherings across the city. He had even published a small book of his works, though it had long been out of print.

"*Phir shaadi hui, bacche hue, zimmedariyan badh gayin*" ~ "Then I got married, had children, responsibilities increased," he explained. "*Mere abbu ki dukaan thi yeh. Unhone mujhe bola, shayari se ghar nahi chalta.*" ~ "This was my father's shop. He told me that poetry doesn't run a household."

So Iqbal set down his pen and picked up his father's scissors. Years passed into decades, and the poet became a barber.

I asked if he was still writing poems.

He paused his work for a moment, his gaze drawn to my reflection in the mirror. Before he continued chopping, he felt something—perhaps pride or longing.

"*Kabhi kabhi, dil karta hai toh likh leta hoon*" ~ "Sometimes, when I feel like it, I write," he admitted. "*Par ab woh sirf mere liye hai. Duniya ke liye nahi.*" ~ "But now it's only for myself. Not for the world."

As he finished my haircut and applied powder to the back of my neck with a delicate brush, I requested if he might share one of his poems.

He paused and then looked around the empty shop. It was late afternoon, the typical lull before the evening rush. Something about my sincere interest must have moved him.

In a voice that abruptly transformed—stronger, more musical, and full of a cadence that hadn't been there before—he recited:

"*Hawa se keh do hum ab bhi zinda hain,*

Baadalon se keh do hum ab bhi barsakte hain."

(Tell the wind that I am still alive,

Tell the clouds that I can still pour.)

The basic lines hung in the air, striking in their directness. I could feel decades of unsaid poetry behind them, a creative spirit that had never fully perished despite being put aside for utilitarian reasons.

As I paid and got ready to go, I told him how great his poetry was. He grinned, and the lines around his eyes deepened.

"*Kala kabhi marti nahi, sahab. Bas kaam ke liye rukti hai,*" (Art never dies, sir. It just pauses for work) he said, sweeping hair clippings from the floor. "*Jaise yeh baal wapas ug jaate hain, waise hi alfaaz bhi.*" (Just as this hair grows back, so do words.)

Walking out of Iqbal Bhai's business, I knew I had gotten much more than just a haircut. I had seen a life that demonstrated how dreams never die; they merely find new expressions. The poet's hands created art with scissors rather than pens, but the artist's soul remained intact.

Dreams may change course from time to time, but they never totally disappear.

The Chair of Vulnerability — Delhi

In Delhi's bustling Paharganj neighborhood, where backpackers and budget travelers mix with locals, I stumbled across a roadside barbershop that was nothing more than a wooden chair under a fading canvas, a small mirror affixed to a tree trunk, and a wooden box carrying the barber's supplies.

The barber, an elderly Sikh man known as Baba ji, had a calm demeanor that stood out against the bustle of Paharganj's main market. His turban was properly knotted, his beard was well-groomed, and his motions were methodical and leisurely, despite the noise and dust swirling about his temporary setup.

As I waited for my turn, I spotted a nicely dressed man seated in the chair. His fancy suit looked out of place in this rustic setting. A gold watch glistened on his wrist, and his spotless leather shoes reflected the afternoon sun.

What struck me the most was that he was crying—quiet tears streamed down his cheeks while Baba ji clipped his hair with basic scissors.

The barber did not appear startled by this. He kept working gently, occasionally resting a loving hand on the man's shoulder, saying nothing but giving comfort with his touch.

When the well-dressed man left, leaving a substantial tip in Baba ji's palm and stroking his feet in reverence, I took my seat, intrigued but apprehensive to inquire about what I had witnessed.

Baba ji began working on my hair, his touch excellent despite his simple instruments. After a few moments of silence, he spoke, as if feeling my unasked query.

"*Beta, sab theek ho jayega,*" (Son, everything will be alright) he said, the same words I had heard him murmur to the crying man.

"*Aapko kaise pata?*" (How do you know?) I asked, surprised.

He smiled gently. "*Aapke liye ya uske liye?*" ~ "For you or for him?"

"*Dono ke liye*" ~ "For both)," I replied.

He nodded, continuing to cut my hair with precise movements.

"*Woh sahab har mahine aate hain. Unki patni ko cancer tha. Pichle saal woh chal basi*" ~ "That gentleman comes every month. His wife had cancer. She passed away last year, he explained quietly. "*Unki patni kehti thi ki mera haircut sabse achha hai. Isliye woh sirf mere paas aate hain, chahe jitni bhi pareshani ho.*" ~ "His wife used to say that my haircut is the best. That's why he only comes to me, no matter how inconvenient it may be.)

I was astonished by how simple the explanation was and how much emotion it communicated. This wealthy businessman went to a modest roadside barber in Paharganj, far from the luxury neighborhoods where he most likely lived, merely to keep this link with his late wife.

"*Kursi pe baithe insaan aksar apne dil ki baat kehte hain*" ~ "People sitting in this chair often speak what's in their hearts)," Baba ji continued, gesturing to the worn wooden seat beneath me. "*Yeh kursi sirf baalon ki katayi ki jagah nahi hai, yeh dukh halka karne ki jagah bhi hai.*" ~ "This chair is not just a place for haircuts; it's a place to lighten sorrows."

In that moment, I understood how rare such venues are in our modern world—places where males may be vulnerable without being judged, and where feelings can be expressed without embarrassment. The barber's chair, with its implicit trust (a guy with a blade at your throat requires faith), fosters a level of intimacy that few other social settings provide.

"*Aap kab se yeh kaam kar rahe hain?*" ~ "How long have you been doing this work?" I asked.

"*Pandrah saal. Pehle main Punjab mein tha. Delhi aaya toh yeh jagah mil gayi*" ~ "Fifteen years. I was previously in Punjab. When I came to Delhi, I found this place," he replied, brushing hair from my shoulders. "*Auron ki kataunis ke saath, unke aansoo bhi kaat deta hoon.*" ~ "Along with cutting their hair, I also cut away their tears."

His metaphor wasn't poetic flourish; it was a sincere description of what I had just witnessed—a man who arrived in grief and left somewhat lightened, not because his problems were solved, but because they had been silently acknowledged and shared.

As Baba ji finished my haircut, I understood that his work went far beyond grooming. In his humble roadside setup, he offered something increasingly rare in our fast-paced world—a moment of genuine human connection, a safe space for vulnerability, a brief respite from the masks men are expected to wear.

The Haircut Before the Interview — Chennai

In Chennai's T. Nagar, I found myself needing a haircut early one morning. The area was already awake and bustling, with shopkeepers arranging their displays and office workers hurrying to catch buses and autos.

I spotted a small barbershop just opening for the day. The barber, an elderly man with a friendly face, was sweeping the floor and setting up his tools. A calendar with colorful images of Hindu deities hung on one wall, and a small shrine with incense occupied a corner of the counter.

"*Welcome, sir. First customer of the day is very good luck,*" he said in English, gesturing to his chair with a smile that crinkled the corners of his eyes.

Everyone called him Murugan Anna (Elder Brother Murugan), and he had been cutting hair in T. Nagar for over thirty years. His shop was simple but spotlessly clean, with two chairs (though he usually worked alone) and a small television mounted in the corner playing Tamil news at low volume.

As he draped the cloth around my shoulders, another customer entered—a young man perhaps in his early twenties, wearing what appeared to be his best shirt and trousers, though they were slightly worn at the edges. His hair was neatly combed but needed trimming, and his expression carried a nervous intensity.

"*Anna, interview ke liye cut chahiye. Jaldi hai*" ~ "Brother, I need a cut for an interview. It's urgent," he said in a mix of Tamil and Hindi.

Seeing his anxiety, Murugan gestured to me with an apologetic look. "*Sir, this boy has an interview. Do you mind waiting?*"

"*Not at all,*" I replied, standing up to give my place.

The young man, who introduced himself as Vimal, sat down with visible tension in his shoulders. As Murugan began to cut his hair, he asked about the interview.

"*Mera pehla job interview hai. IT company mein*" ~ "It's my first job interview. At an IT company," Vimal explained, his fingers nervously tapping the armrests. "*Maine engineering complete ki hai, lekin family mein koi professional nahi hai. Mujhe nahi pata kya expect karoon.*" ~ "I've completed engineering, but no one in my family is a professional. I don't know what to expect."

He was the first in his family to graduate from college, he explained. His father was a construction worker, his mother a house cleaner. They had sacrificed everything to put him through engineering school, working double shifts and borrowing money from relatives.

"*Agar yeh job nahi mila toh... main unka sapna tod dunga*" ~ "If I don't get this job... I'll break their dream," he said, his voice catching slightly.

Murugan listened silently as he worked, his experienced hands moving swiftly but carefully around Vimal's head.

When he finished the cut, he did something I hadn't seen a barber do before—he spent extra time styling Vimal's hair, using a small amount of gel to give it a professional look.

"*Idhar aao, beta*" ~ "Come here, son," Murugan said, turning Vimal to face the mirror directly. He placed his hands on the young man's shoulders and spoke in a mixture of Tamil and Hindi that I could only partially understand, but the essence was clear.

He was telling Vimal to stand straight, to remember his parents' sacrifices but not let them become a burden, and to speak with confidence because he had earned his place in that interview room. As Vimal listened, his posture gradually changed—his shoulders straightened, and his chin lifted slightly.

Before Vimal left, Murugan tied a sacred thread around his wrist—something usually done at temples for blessing—and refused to accept payment.

"*Pehle naukri lo, phir aana*" ~ "First get the job, then come back," he said with a smile. "*Ab jao, interview jeet lo.*" ~ "Now go, win your interview."

I watched as Vimal walked out of the shop, his bearing transformed not just by the haircut but by something more profound— the blessing of confidence, the knowledge that someone believed in him.

Later that day, after completing some errands in T. Nagar, I passed by Murugan's shop again. To my surprise, I saw Vimal there, his face lit with excitement. He was showing Murugan a letter— presumably a job offer—and the old barber was beaming with pride.

"*Bhaiyya, main select ho gaya!*" ~ "Brother, I got selected!" Vimal exclaimed when he saw me.

Murugan winked at me. "*Ek achha haircut insaan ko badal sakta hai!*" ~ "A good haircut can change a person!"

We all knew it wasn't just the haircut. It was the moment of human connection, the transfer of confidence, the simple act of one man believing in another. In that small Chennai barbershop, I had witnessed a transformation more significant than mere appearance—I had seen a young man step into his future with newfound assurance.

Dignity in a Simple Shave — Kolkata

During my time in Kolkata, I was walking through the Esplanade area one evening when I noticed a scene that stopped me in my tracks.

A homeless man stood outside a small barbershop, staring through the window. His clothes were tattered, his beard long and unkempt, and his possessions were contained in a single cloth bag slung over his shoulder. But what caught my attention was the longing in his gaze as he watched the barber inside working on a customer.

The barbershop was modest but proper—three chairs, mirrors, and a glass counter displaying combs, scissors, and hair products. The owner, a middle-aged Bengali man with salt-and-pepper hair, noticed the homeless man outside and, to my surprise, gestured for him to come in.

I moved closer, curious about the interaction. The homeless man hesitated at the doorway.

"*Paise nahi hain*" ~ "I don't have money," he said, his voice rough from disuse.

The barber waved dismissively. "*Paise baad mein de dena. Pehle shave toh kara lo.*" ~ "Pay me later. First, get a shave."

With uncertain steps, the homeless man entered and sat in an empty chair. The barber draped him with a clean cloth, just as he would any paying customer, and began preparing hot towels and shaving cream.

I took a seat on a bench outside, pretending to check my phone but actually watching this unexpected scene unfold through the open door.

The transformation was remarkable. As the barber worked, removing weeks of beard growth with careful strokes, the homeless man's features emerged—a strong jawline, high cheekbones, and expressive eyes that had been partially hidden by the wild growth of facial hair. With each pass of the razor, he seemed to straighten a little more in the chair, his dignity visibly returning.

The barber worked silently, with the same care and attention he would give to any customer. He applied aftershave, combed the man's hair, and even trimmed his eyebrows. Throughout the process, he maintained a professional demeanor—no pity, no condescension, just the respect of one human being for another.

When the shave was complete, the homeless man touched his smooth face with wonder, as if rediscovering a part of himself long forgotten. He looked at his reflection for a long moment, something close to a smile lifting the corners of his mouth.

He stood and folded his hands in gratitude. "*Dhanyavaad*" ~ "Thank you," he whispered, his voice carrying a weight of emotion beyond the simple word.

As he turned to leave, he reached into his bag, apparently searching for something to offer as payment. The barber shook his head.

"*Aaj nahi. Jab aapke paas ho, tab de dena*" ~ "Not today. When you have it, you can pay," he said.

After the homeless man left, I entered the shop for my own haircut. As the barber worked, I couldn't help asking why he had offered a free service to a man who might never be able to pay.

He looked at me through the mirror, his expression thoughtful.

"*Koi bhi aadmi achha dikhna chahta hai, babu. Gareebi iska matlab nahi ki insaan apni izzat kho de*" ~ "Every man wants to look good. Poverty doesn't mean losing one's dignity," he said simply. "*Kabhi kabhi, ek clean shave se zyada zaroorat nahi hoti apne aap ko phir se dhoondhne ke liye.*" ~ "Sometimes, nothing more than a clean shave is needed to find oneself again."

His words stayed with me long after I left his shop. In a world obsessed with status and appearance, this barber understood something profound—that looking good isn't just a luxury for the privileged; it's a basic human desire tied to our sense of self-worth.

By treating the homeless man with the same respect he showed his paying customers, by refusing to let poverty strip away the man's right to dignity, the barber had performed an act of kindness far more meaningful than mere charity. He had acknowledged man's humanity in a world that too often rendered him invisible.

Temples of Transformation

As I traveled across India, from the crowded lanes of Mumbai to the busy streets of Kolkata, I found that barbershops served as more than just places for grooming. They were temples of transformation, where people came not just to change their appearance but to rediscover parts of themselves.

I encountered:

- A poet who found a different expression for his creativity
- A grieving widower seeking connection to his lost love
- A nervous graduate gaining confidence for his future
- A homeless man reclaiming his dignity

In each case, the barber was more than just a service provider—he was a silent confidant, an unofficial therapist, a witness to vulnerability, and sometimes, a source of wisdom and encouragement.

What makes barbershops unique in our fast-paced digital world is that they require something increasingly rare—human pause. You cannot get a haircut while rushing to your next appointment. You must sit still, surrender control, and engage in that most endangered of activities: face-to-face conversation without screens between you.

In these humble establishments, with their simple chairs and basic tools, I found a reminder of what we often lose in our pursuit of efficiency and convenience—the profound value of human touch, the comfort of shared silence, and the transformative power of being truly seen by another person.

The next time you sit in a barber's chair, look around. You might be witnessing small acts of humanity that go far beyond a haircut—a man finally sharing his grief, a young person gaining confidence before a life-changing event, or a forgotten individual reclaiming their dignity.

In a world where we are increasingly isolated by technology and divided by differences, the barbershop remains a rare democratic space—where everyone, regardless of status, sits in the same chair, looks into the same mirror, and for a brief moment, shows the same vulnerability.

And perhaps that is the greatest service barbers provide—not the haircuts themselves, but the space for us to be human together, if only for thirty minutes in a busy day.

Chapter 9:
Tea Stalls: The Unofficial Town Squares

The Heartbeat of India

If India has a pulse, it can be found in its tea stalls.

From the snow-capped mountains of Himachal to the backwaters of Kerala, from the deserts of Rajasthan to the beaches of Odisha—wherever you go in this vast country, you will find a chai stall. They dot highways, railway platforms, street corners, and marketplaces, appearing wherever people gather, rest, or wait.

These are not just places to drink tea. They are India's unofficial town squares—where strangers become friends, where politics is debated with passion, where hearts are broken and mended, where deals are struck, and where life unfolds in all its messy, beautiful complexity.

I had passed thousands of tea stalls in my life, often glimpsing them through tinted car windows. As a corporate executive, I occasionally indulged in "cutting chai" during field visits, considering it a cultural experience rather than an everyday habit. But after selling my Mercedes and stepping into the real world, tea stalls became my classrooms, my rest stops, and my windows into lives I had never truly seen before.

This chapter isn't about the tea itself—though there's an art to the perfect balance of tea leaves, milk, sugar, and spices. This is about the people who pour their hearts out alongside the steaming chai, the conversations that brew longer than the tea, and the human connections that form over small glass cups shared in moments of pause.

The Midnight Chaiwala of Marine Drive — Mumbai

It was well past midnight when I found myself walking along Mumbai's famous Marine Drive. The "Queen's Necklace"—a curved string of lights along the promenade—shimmered on one side, while the vast Arabian Sea stretched into darkness on the other. The daytime chaos of Mumbai had subsided to a gentle hum, with only occasional cars passing by and a few couples sitting on the concrete barrier, whispering to each other under the stars.

As I walked, feeling both the freedom and loneliness that nighttime in a big city brings, I noticed a small flickering light ahead. It came from a modest tea stall—nothing more than a wooden cart with a gas stove, a large aluminum kettle, and a few small stools arranged around it.

The vendor was an older man, perhaps in his late fifties, with deep lines etched into his face and hands that showed years of labor. Despite the late hour, he moved with purpose and energy, brewing fresh tea in his large kettle. A small kerosene lamp illuminated his workspace, casting warm golden light that created a circle of comfort in the darkness.

Around his stall sat five or six people—a couple of taxi drivers taking a break from their night shifts, an office watchman in uniform, a young woman who looked like she might work at a call center, and a middle-aged man staring silently at the sea.

I approached, drawn by both the aroma of cardamom-infused chai and the small island of humanity on the otherwise empty night.

"*Ek chai, bhaiya,*" (One tea, brother) I requested, taking a seat on an empty wooden stool.

The chai vendor—whom everyone called **Prakash**—poured the steaming tea into a small glass with practiced precision, creating a perfect arc of liquid without spilling a drop. His movements were efficient yet unhurried, suggesting someone who had performed this ritual thousands of times.

"*Pehli baar itni raat ko Marine Drive pe?*" (First time on Marine Drive so late at night?) he asked with a knowing smile as he handed me the glass.

I nodded, surprised by his perceptiveness.

"*Yahan raat ko duniya alag hoti hai*" ~ "The world is different here at night," he said, returning to his kettle to prepare more tea. "*Din ka Mumbai aur raat ka Mumbai—bilkul alag shaher hain.*" "Day Mumbai and night Mumbai—completely different cities."

As I sipped the strong, sweet tea, I observed the little community that had formed around Prakash's cart. The taxi drivers were discussing rising fuel costs and decreasing earnings. The watchman sat in tired silence, occasionally checking his watch. The young woman was on her phone, perhaps coordinating her ride home after a late shift.

One of the taxi drivers noticed my observation and smiled. "*Prakash bhai ka chai sabse achha hai, aur unka dil bhi. Kai baar paise nahi hote, phir bhi pilate hain.*" ~ "Prakash brother's tea is the best, and so is his heart. Many times, we don't have money, still he serves us."

I turned to Prakash. "*Aap raat bhar kaam karte ho?*" ~ "Do you work all night?"

His weathered face crinkled in a smile that reached his kind eyes. "*Raat ke log alag hote hain, sahab. Yeh unki chai hai.*" (The night people are different, sir. This is their tea.)

He explained how he had been setting up his stall at this same spot for nearly twenty years, serving from 10 PM until 5 AM. His customers were taxi and auto drivers, security guards, hospital staff taking breaks, night shift workers from call centers and hotels, and occasionally, insomniacs, heartbroken lovers, or visitors like me who found themselves awake while the city slept.

"*Kisi ki raat sirf sona hoti hai, aur kisi ki raat poori zindagi hoti hai*" ~ "For some, the night is just for sleeping, but for others, it's an entire life," he said, his simple words carrying profound understanding.

As he spoke, a man approached—disheveled, slightly intoxicated, with red-rimmed eyes that suggested recent tears. Without a word, Prakash poured him tea and placed two biscuits on the saucer. No money changed hands.

Later, when the man left and I questioned this, Prakash shrugged. "*Uski biwi chhod gayi do hafte pehle. Ab woh har raat idhar aata hai. Kabhi paise deta hai, kabhi nahi. Par chai se neend nahi aati, dard thoda kam hota hai.*" ~ "His wife left him two weeks ago. Now he comes here every night. Sometimes he pays, sometimes not. Tea doesn't bring sleep, but it reduces the pain a little."

I stayed at Prakash's stall for over an hour, watching this night guardian of Marine Drive serve not just tea but momentary comfort to Mumbai's nocturnal souls. In his small circle of lantern light, I saw a microcosm of urban isolation and the small, vital connections that help people survive it.

Before leaving, I asked him why he chose to work nights instead of days when business might be better.

"*Din mein chai bechne wale hazaron hain*" ~ "There are thousands selling tea during the day," he replied, wiping his hands on a cloth. "*Raat mein kuch hi log hain jo jagte hain aur serve karte hain. Mujhe lagta hai ki isme thodi si zaroorat hai, toh main kar leta hoon.*" ~ "At night, there are few who stay awake and serve. I feel there's a small need for this, so I do it."

As I walked away, his stall's small light continued to flicker behind me— a tiny lighthouse guiding night travelers to a moment of pause, warmth, and human acknowledgment in the vast darkness of the sleeping city.

The Man Who Found Life in a Delhi Tea Stall

In Old Delhi's chaotic Chandni Chowk, a stone's throw from the majestic Jama Masjid, I discovered a bustling tea stall wedged between a spice shop and a textile store. Unlike Prakash's solitary nighttime operation, this was a place of constant motion and noise— a chorus of voices arguing politics, discussing cricket scores, and haggling over business deals, all while jostling for space in the narrow lane.

The stall itself was slightly more established— a permanent structure with a small counter, shelves stocked with biscuit packets and savory snacks, and a large sign proudly proclaiming, *"Purani Dilli Ki Mashoor Wali Chai"* ~ "Old Delhi's Famous Tea". Three giant kettles boiled simultaneously on gas burners, tended by a team of young helpers who moved with remarkable coordination in the tiny space.

The owner, Karim Chacha (Uncle Karim), was a jovial man with a large mustache and an even larger voice that somehow carried over the market's din. He remembered regular customers' preferences, called out greetings to passersby, and kept a watchful eye on his assistants, all while maintaining a running commentary on everything from the weather to the government's latest policies.

"*Arey sahab, naya chehra! Pehli baar hamari chai peene aaye ho?*" ~ "Oh sir, a new face! First time trying our tea?" he called out when he spotted me hesitating near his stall.

I nodded and asked for a masala chai, which arrived in a small clay cup that felt warm against my palms. The first sip revealed a perfect balance of strong tea, creamy milk, cardamom, ginger, and just enough sugar to complement the spices without overwhelming them.

Standing near the stall, I observed the diverse clientele—shopkeepers taking brief breaks, tourists exploring Old Delhi, laborers pausing for refreshment, and businessmen in formal attire who had clearly traveled from other parts of the city specifically for this chai.

Amid this varied crowd, one figure stood out: an elderly man in a faded but immaculately pressed Nehru jacket, sitting alone on a small bench attached to the side of the stall. Unlike the others who came and went quickly, he seemed settled, as if the bench were reserved for him. He sipped his tea slowly, gazing into the distance with eyes that registered the bustle around him but didn't participate in it.

When I asked Karim Chacha about him, his usual boisterous manner softened.

"*Woh Sharma ji hain*" ~ "That's Mr. Sharma," he said, lowering his voice slightly. "*Pichle bees saal se har din aate hain, same time, same bench.*" ~ "For the past twenty years, he comes every day, same time, same bench."

The story emerged gradually. Mr. Sharma had once been a government officer with a comfortable life, a respected position, and a loving family. But twenty years ago, a terrible accident had claimed the lives of his wife and son while he was away on work. The tragedy had shattered him completely.

"*Us din se, ghar mein akela baithna bardasht nahi hota*" ~ "Since that day, he cannot bear sitting alone at home," Karim explained. "*Yeh jagah mujhe akela mehsoos nahi hone deti.*" ~ "This place doesn't let him feel alone."

Every day for two decades, Mr. Sharma had been coming to this tea stall. He would sit for exactly one hour, drink two cups of tea, occasionally nod to regulars he recognized, and then leave—a ritual as precise and unchanging as the hands of a clock.

"*Kabhi baat nahi karte?*" ~ "He never talks?" I asked.

"*Kabhi kabhi, kisi special din pe. Jaise unki biwi ka birthday, ya bete ki anniversary. Tab thodi baat karte hain, purani yaadein share karte hain*" ~ "Sometimes, on special days. Like his wife's birthday or son's anniversary. Then he talks a little, shares old memories," Karim said. "*Baaki din bas chai peete hain, logon ko dekhte hain, zinda mehsoos karte hain.*" ~ "Other days he just drinks tea, watches people, feels alive."

Later, I gathered the courage to sit beside Mr. Sharma. For several minutes, we sat in silence, watching the chaotic ballet of Old Delhi life unfold before us—cycle rickshaws navigating impossible spaces, children running errands for their parents' shops, tourists photographing the centuries-old buildings.

Finally, he spoke, his voice surprisingly clear and strong: "*Acha lagta hai, logon ko dekh ke. Unki zindagi mein thodi der ke liye shaamil ho jaana.*" ~ "It feels good, watching people. Becoming part of their lives for a little while."

It was the only thing he said to me, but it carried the weight of twenty years of silent observation, of finding reasons to continue when all personal connections had been severed. In this bustling tea stall, surrounded by strangers too busy to notice his grief, he had found a way to remain tethered to the world.

As I left Karim's stall that day, I realized that for some people, places like these weren't just about refreshment—they were lifelines, thin threads connecting them to humanity when all other bonds had been cut. A simple chai stall had quite literally saved a man's life by giving him somewhere to be, something to do, and people to observe day after day for twenty years.

The Engineer Who Found Pride in Pouring Tea — Chennai

In Chennai's T. Nagar, amid the morning rush of office-goers and the opening of textile shops, I came across a tea stall that immediately stood out from the others dotting the busy commercial area.

The small shop was unusually tidy—its counter polished, its glasses spotlessly clean, its sign hand-painted in bold blue letters: "**Smart Chai: Taste the Success**." The vendor, a young man perhaps in his mid-twenties, wore a crisp white shirt and had his hair neatly combed, looking more like a bank clerk than a tea seller.

This contrast to the typical image of a tea vendor—usually an older man in casual clothes working from a makeshift setup—caught my attention. I joined the small line of customers and observed how he worked with methodical precision, measuring ingredients exactly, timing each brew with a small kitchen timer, and serving with a flourish that turned the simple act of pouring tea into a performance.

"*Ek chai*" ~ "One tea," I requested when my turn came.

"*Special chai, filter coffee, green tea, ya lemon tea?*" he replied with a professional smile, listing options I hadn't expected at a roadside stall.

I chose the special chai and watched as he prepared it with theatrical flair, stretching the tea between two containers in a long, perfect pour that reminded me of the famous "meter coffee" of Tamil Nadu.

"*Aap kab se yeh stall chala rahe hain?*" ~ "How long have you been running this stall?" I asked as he handed me my tea.

"*Sirf do saal,*" ~ "Only two years," he replied. "*Pehle kuch aur karta tha.*" ~ "I used to do something else."

His name was Rajesh, and as the morning rush subsided, he shared his story. He was an engineering graduate who had spent two years searching unsuccessfully for a job in his field. With student loans to repay and family responsibilities mounting, the pressure had become unbearable.

"*Har interview mein same story—experience chahiye, fresher ko chance nahi*" ~ "Every interview was the same story—they want experience, no chance for freshers," he explained. "*Mere classmates mein se aadhe abhi bhi berozgaar hain, ya phir minimum wage pe kaam kar rahe hain jisme degree ki zaroorat hi nahi.*" ~ "Half my classmates are still unemployed or working minimum wage jobs that don't even require a degree."

Initially, he felt deep shame at the prospect of becoming a tea vendor after his parents had sacrificed so much for his education. His father, a bus conductor, and his mother, a tailor, had invested their life savings to send him to an engineering college.

"*Mai depression mein tha. Engineering graduate hokar chai bechna? Log kya kahenge?*" ~ "I was depressed. Selling tea after becoming an engineering graduate? What would people say?" he said, his expression momentarily clouding.

But necessity drove him to start small, with just a kettle and a few glasses. And then something unexpected happened: he began applying his engineering mindset to the business of selling tea.

"*Maine socha, agar chai hi bechna hai, toh sabse achhi chai kyun na bechuun? Systematic approach, quality control, innovation—engineering concepts jo maine college mein seekhe the, sab apply kiye.*" ~ "I thought, if I must sell tea, why not sell the best tea? Systematic approach, quality control, innovation—I applied engineering concepts I learned in college."

He researched tea varieties, experimented with recipes, calculated the precise temperature for optimal extraction, and analyzed customer preferences. He designed his stall for maximum efficiency, timed his processes to eliminate waste, and branded his business to stand out in the crowded market.

With a touch of humor, he rebranded his stall as providing "MBA Chai"—where MBA stood for "**M**arketing, **B**usiness, and **A**ttitude." What began as a desperate fallback had transformed into a thriving small business that now employed two other struggling graduates.

"*Ab main coffee shop kholne ka plan kar raha hoon*" ~ "Now I'm planning to open a coffee shop," he said with evident pride. "*Phir franchises, phir maybe food business. Engineering mein job nahi mili, toh kya hua? Entrepreneur ban gaya.*" ~ "Then franchises, then maybe food business. I didn't get an engineering job, so what? I became an entrepreneur."

What struck me most about Rajesh was how he had transformed stigma into pride. He had taken the work that society deemed beneath his education and elevated it through excellence and innovation. His story challenged my own preconceptions about success and status— reminding me that dignity comes not from what work you do, but how you do it.

As new customers arrived and Rajesh returned to his choreographed tea-making, I observed the respect with which people treated him. They weren't just buying tea; they were buying into his vision, his story of reinvention.

In a country obsessed with prestigious degrees and traditional career paths, Rajesh's tea stall stood as a quiet revolution—proving that true education reveals itself not in job titles but in the ability to adapt, innovate, and find pride in whatever path life presents.

The Women's Circle at Park Street — Kolkata

On a rainy afternoon in Kolkata, I ducked into a small tea shop on Park Street to escape a sudden downpour. Unlike the open stalls I had visited in other cities, this was a proper shop with walls, a tin roof, and several small tables with wooden benches. The windows were fogged from the steam of brewing tea, creating a cozy atmosphere set against the rhythm of raindrops on the roof.

What immediately caught my attention wasn't the décor or the menu but a group of six women in colorful sarees, occupying the largest table in the corner. They ranged in age from perhaps thirty to sixty, and their animated conversation punctuated by bursts of laughter stood out in a space otherwise dominated by men quietly reading newspapers or having hushed conversations.

The owner, a Bengali man with thick glasses who introduced himself as Bannerjee-da, served me a cup of Darjeeling tea and noticed my interest in the women's group.

"*Ora prottek sombar ase*" ~ "They come every Monday," he explained in Bengali, then switched to Hindi seeing my confusion. "*Pichle paanch saal se, same time, same table.*" ~ "For the past five years, same time, same table."

He explained that they had started as just two women—neighbors who would meet for tea while their husbands were at work. Gradually, others joined, and it became a weekly ritual—their "Women's Tea Parliament," as Bannerjee-da called it with affectionate amusement.

"*Shunte hain Bangla politics se lekar America ke president tak, sab kuch pe baat hoti hai*" ~ "I hear they talk about everything from Bengali politics to America's president," he chuckled. "*Mere shop ko United Nations bana diya hai.*" ~ "They've turned my shop into the United Nations."

As the afternoon progressed and the rain continued to fall, I couldn't help overhearing snippets of their wide-ranging conversation—which jumped from local community issues to their children's education, from book recommendations to recipes, from social issues to personal challenges.

When two of the women left, I gathered my courage and approached the remaining four, introducing myself and asking if I could join them briefly to learn about their gathering.

They welcomed me with immediate warmth, pulling out a chair and offering me a samosa from their shared plate. The informal leader of the group appeared to be Malati-di, a poised woman in her fifties with graying hair and intelligent eyes behind red-framed glasses.

"*Hum log bas chai peene aate hain, aur zindagi ke bare mein baat karte hain*" ~ "We just come to drink tea and talk about life," she explained with elegant simplicity. "*Ghar ke andar auraton ki baat sunne wala kam hota hai. Yahan ham khud ko sunte hain.*" ~ "Inside the home, there are few who listen to women. Here, we listen to ourselves."

Another woman, perhaps in her late thirties, who introduced herself as Lakshmi, added: "*Mere pati kehte hain ki auraton ko itna bolna nahi chahiye. Lekin yahan koi tokta nahi.*" ~ "My husband says women shouldn't talk so much. But here, no one interrupts."

As they shared more, I learned that their weekly meetings had grown beyond social connection into something more purposeful. They had started a small lending circle to help each other through financial difficulties. They exchanged information about educational opportunities for their children. They discussed healthcare issues that women often felt uncomfortable raising with male doctors.

But most importantly, they had created a space where their voices mattered—where they could express opinions on everything from domestic politics to international affairs without being dismissed or talked over.

The quietest member of the group, Sumitra, who had barely spoken since I joined them, suddenly shared something that captured the essence of what this tea shop meant to them:

"*Pehli baar yahan aane ke baad, mujhe laga ki meri baat bhi matter karti hai*" ~ "After coming here for the first time, I felt that my words mattered too," she said, her soft voice gaining strength as she spoke. "*Ab main ghar pe bhi bolti hoon.*

Pehle sirf sunti thi." ~ "Now I speak at home too. Before, I only listened."

The rain eventually stopped, and as the women prepared to leave—each returning to homes where they were mothers, wives, daughters-in-law with defined roles and responsibilities—I saw a subtle transformation in their bearing. They walked out not as subdued women seeking temporary escape, but as individuals who had been affirmed, who had spoken and been heard.

Bannerjee-da, clearing their cups after they left, shared a final observation: "*Chai ki dukan sirf chai nahi bechti. Thodi si jagah bhi bechti hai jahan log woh ban sakte hain jo ghar pe nahi ban sakte.*" ~ "A tea shop doesn't just sell tea. It also sells a small space where people can be what they cannot be at home."

The Bridges Between Strangers

Tea stalls across India serve as more than just places to quench thirst. They are bridges between strangers, pause buttons in chaotic lives, and safe spaces for authentic expression.

I had witnessed:

- A midnight guardian serving warmth to Mumbai's nocturnal souls
- An elderly man finding connection to life through daily ritual
- A young engineer transforming necessity into entrepreneurial pride
- Women creating a space for their voices in a society that often silenced them

Unlike restaurants where the bill creates pressure to leave, or bars where social expectations dictate behavior, tea stalls offer a rare democracy of space—where for the price of a small cup, anyone can claim temporary citizenship in a community.

From the mountains of Darjeeling to the deserts of Jaisalmer, from dawn till well past midnight, India's countless tea vendors do more than serve beverages. They create the essential third spaces— neither home nor workplace—where society breathes, where strangers become acquaintances, and where the true pulse of a community can be felt.

The humble chai stall, with its small glasses and sweet, milky brew, forms the backdrop against which many of life's significant moments unfold—business deals and breakups, political awakening and personal revelation, friendship formation and conflict resolution.

In our increasingly digital age, where connections are often mediated through screens and algorithms, these physical gathering places remind us of the irreplaceable value of face-to-face interaction, of conversation unfiltered by technology, of community formed through physical presence rather than virtual proximity.

So, the next time you pass a roadside tea stall—whether it's an elaborate setup with benches and tables or just a single kettle on a wooden cart—remember that you're looking at more than a business. You're seeing one of India's true democratic institutions, a place where stories brew alongside the tea, where strangers find common ground over small glass cups, and where—sip by sip—the social fabric of the country is continuously rewoven.

As the Tamil proverb goes: "*Kaiyil oru kopai chaya, kadaiyil oru nimisham nillu, nanbatvam irukattum, nanmai irukattum.*" ~ "A cup of tea in hand, a minute's pause at the shop, let there be friendship, let there be goodness."

Chapter 10:
The Faces of Faith

Beyond Temples and Rituals

Faith is not always found where we expect it.

Growing up, I had a simple understanding of religion—it was about temples and mosques, churches and gurudwaras, rituals and prayers. Faith seemed to exist primarily within institutional boundaries, clearly labeled and neatly categorized.

But as I traveled across India after selling my Mercedes, I discovered that faith wears many faces—some of them surprising, some contradictory, and some profoundly moving in their simplicity.

I met devout believers who had never entered a house of worship. I encountered religious leaders whose true devotion was to humanity rather than dogma. I witnessed acts of profound faith that had nothing to do with gods or scriptures.

What I learned is that faith exists not just in grand gestures or ancient rituals, but in the small, quiet moments of human connection—in acts of kindness that transcend religious boundaries, in courage found when all else is lost, and in the resilience of the human spirit when faced with life's greatest challenges.

This chapter isn't about religion as an institution. It's about faith as a living force in the lives of ordinary people— both those who profess deep religious beliefs and those who claim none at all.

The Priest Who Saved a Muslim Life — Hyderabad

In the heart of Hyderabad's Old City, near the historic Charminar, stands a small but vibrant Hindu temple dedicated to Lord Ganesh. Its modest structure, sandwiched between shops selling bangles and perfumes, belies its importance to the local Hindu community, who stream in throughout the day to offer prayers.

The temple's head priest, Pandit Hari Prasad, was a man in his sixties with a gentle voice and kind eyes that crinkled at the corners when he smiled. When I first visited, he was performing the evening aarti—waving a lamp in circular motions before the deity while chanting mantras in his melodious voice. Devotees stood with folded hands, some with eyes closed in deep meditation, others singing along with the priest.

The atmosphere was one of devotion and peace— the scent of incense filling the air, the sound of bells mingling with the chanting, the golden glow of oil lamps illuminating the sanctum.

After the ceremony concluded and most worshippers had left, I approached Pandit Hari Prasad to learn more about the temple's history. But our conversation took an unexpected turn when a commotion erupted at the temple entrance.

A Muslim family—a woman in a black burqa, two small children, and an elderly man—were being stopped by the temple caretaker. The woman was speaking rapidly in a mix of Urdu and Telugu, her voice rising with desperation.

Though I couldn't understand her words, the urgency in her tone was unmistakable.

Without hesitation, Pandit Hari Prasad hurried over. The caretaker explained that the family was Muslim and had come seeking the priest specifically, not to worship.

"*Koi baat nahi. Andar aane do*" ~ "It doesn't matter. Let them in," he said firmly, gesturing for the family to enter.

The woman immediately fell at his feet, sobbing. Through her tears, she explained their situation. Her husband, the family's sole breadwinner, had been diagnosed with a rare blood disease. He needed multiple transfusions of a particularly uncommon blood type, and despite searching for weeks, they had found no matching donors. Someone had told her that Pandit ji had helped other families in similar situations.

The priest listened patiently, then took out a small notebook and asked for details—the hospital, the patient's name, blood type, and how many units were needed.

"*Fikar mat kijiye, behan. Hum kuch karenge*" ~ "Don't worry, sister. We will do something," he assured her.

After they left, I couldn't contain my curiosity. "Will you perform a special puja for them?" I asked, assuming his help would be spiritual in nature.

He smiled. "*Puja se khoon nahi milta, beta. Action lena padta hai.*" ~ "Blood doesn't come from prayer, son. Action must be taken."

He explained that over the years, he had built a network of blood donors from among the temple's congregation and beyond. Whenever someone needed a rare blood type, he would mobilize this network, sending messages through devotees and making announcements after temple ceremonies.

"*But they're Muslim*," I said, immediately regretting my words and the assumptions they revealed.

The priest looked at me, not with anger but with genuine puzzlement.

"*To? Khoon mein kaunsa dharm hota hai? Hindu khoon, Muslim khoon?*" ~ "So? Which religion does blood have? Hindu blood, Muslim blood?" he asked. "*Sab ka khoon laal hi hota hai.*" ~ "Everyone's blood is red."

The next morning, I returned to the temple to find Pandit Hari Prasad addressing a small crowd after the morning aarti. He was explaining the Muslim family's situation and calling for blood donors of the matching type. Some devotees looked uncomfortable; a few even walked away.

"*Kuch log sochte hain ki yeh hamare dharm ke khilaaf hai*" ~ "Some people think this is against our religion," he acknowledged when he saw their reaction. "*Par agar hum bhagwan ke bhakt hain, toh insaaniyat sabse bada dharm hai.*" ~ "But if we are devotees of God, then humanity is the greatest religion."

His words were simple but powerful. By the end of the day, several devotees had volunteered to be tested as potential donors. Within a week, enough matching donors had been found for the critically ill man to receive his needed transfusions.

A month later, when I visited the temple again before leaving Hyderabad, I witnessed an extraordinary scene. The Muslim family had returned—this time with the father, still weak but recovering. They stood hesitantly at the temple entrance until Pandit Hari Prasad spotted them and welcomed them warmly.

The man tried to touch the priest's feet in gratitude, but Pandit ji stopped him and instead embraced him like a brother. No words were exchanged; none were needed. As the family left, the temple bells seemed to ring with particular clarity, as if in approval of this moment that transcended religious boundaries.

That day, I realized that true faith isn't confined to rituals or buildings. Sometimes it manifests in the simple recognition of our shared humanity— in seeing beyond labels to the universal needs and hopes that connect us all.

The Man Who Had No God — Varanasi

If there is a city in India where religion permeates every aspect of life, it is Varanasi. Known as the spiritual capital of India, this ancient city on the banks of the Ganges is a place where life and death play out in public view, where cremation pyres burn continuously, and where pilgrims come from across the country to bathe in the sacred river.

I arrived in Varanasi at dawn, when the city is at its most magical. A light mist hovered over the Ganges, and the rising sun cast a golden glow on the ancient temples and buildings lining the riverbank. The ghats—stone steps leading down to the water—were already coming alive with activity: priests performing morning rituals, devotees taking ritual baths, yoga practitioners greeting the sun, and tourists capturing the ethereal scene with their cameras.

Amid this spiritual panorama, I noticed a solitary figure sitting cross-legged on a small wooden platform near Dashashwamedh Ghat. He was an elderly man with a long white beard and sinewy limbs, dressed simply in a white dhoti. His eyes were closed, his back perfectly straight, and his hands rested palms-up on his knees. He seemed completely immersed in meditation, oblivious to the activity around him.

Unlike the other sadhus who occasionally posed for photographs with tourists in exchange for donations, this man had no trappings of religious display—no tilak on his forehead, no rudraksha beads, no pictures of deities. Just a profound stillness that drew my attention amid the bustling ghat.

Day after day during my stay in Varanasi, I would see him at the same spot, in the same position, displaying the same intense focus. Curiosity finally overcame my hesitation to disturb his meditation. One morning, I sat quietly nearby, waiting until his eyes opened before speaking.

"*Namaste, baba. Aap roz yahan dhyan lagate hain?*" ~ "Greetings, respected one. Do you meditate here every day?" I asked.

He turned to me with clear, alert eyes that seemed to see beyond the surface. "*Tees saal se. Har din.*" ~ "For thirty years. Every day."

Thirty years of daily meditation in the same spot—the dedication was astounding. I asked if he was a devoted follower of a particular deity or guru.

His answer stunned me.

"*Mere paas koi bhagwan nahi hai.*" ~ "I have no god."

In Varanasi, the holiest city for Hindus, surrounded by thousands of temples and shrines, this statement was extraordinary. I must have looked shocked because he smiled slightly.

"*Ajeeb laga?*" "Seems strange?" he asked.

I nodded, and he gestured for me to sit beside him. As the morning light strengthened and pilgrims continued their rituals in the sacred river below us, he shared his story.

"*Beta, zindagi ne mujhe har baar giraya. Maine bhagwan se madad maangi, par kuch nahi mila. Fir maine apni aatma ko bhagwan mana, aur jeevan badal gaya.*" (Son, life knocked me down again and again. I asked God for help, but nothing changed. Then, I started treating my own soul as God, and my life changed.)

He had once been a wealthy landowner with a family and position in society. A series of calamities—a flood that destroyed his crops, a dishonest business partner who stole his savings, and the death of his wife and son from illness—had stripped him of everything. In desperation, he had come to Varanasi, the city of salvation, praying at every temple, performing every ritual, and seeking divine intervention.

"*Maine apna sab kuch bhagwan ko de diya, par bhagwan ne mujhe kuch nahi diya.*" ~ "I gave everything to God, but God gave me nothing in return." His voice held no bitterness, only the calm clarity of someone stating facts.

At his lowest point, contemplating ending his life in the Ganges, he had an epiphany: perhaps the divine wasn't external but within. Perhaps the strength he sought wasn't going to come from above but from deep inside himself.

That realization began his true spiritual journey—not one of devotion to deities or adherence to rituals, but of discovering his inner resources, the resilience of his own spirit, the divinity within his humanity.

"*Ab main bahar nahi, andar dekhta hoon. Shakti wahaan hai.*" ~ "Now I look inward, not outward. That's where the power is."

For thirty years, he had meditated on the ghat, not to communicate with gods but to connect more deeply with himself. His spiritual practice was entirely self-directed, focused on cultivating inner strength, peace, and wisdom.

"*Aapko dharm ki zaroorat nahi lagti?*" ~ "Don't you feel the need for religion?" I asked, still trying to understand his perspective.

He gestured toward the river, where people were immersing themselves in the sacred waters with expressions of devotion and hope.

"*Dharm alag cheez hai, vishwas alag. In logon ko vishwas chahiye ki koi unki madad karega. Mujhe vishwas hai ki main khud kar sakta hoon.*" ~ "Religion is one thing, faith is another. These people need to believe someone will help them. I believe I can help myself."

As I left him to his meditation, his words echoed in my mind. Here was a man who had abandoned traditional religiosity yet embodied a profound faith—not in external powers but in the strength of the human spirit. In one of India's most religious cities, he had found a personal spirituality that required no temples, no rituals, no gods—only the quiet conviction that divinity resided within.

His story reminded me that faith comes in many forms, and sometimes the most powerful beliefs are those we discover not through doctrine but through our own experiences of loss, resilience, and renewal.

The Muslim Who Rebuilt a Hindu Temple — Lucknow

Lucknow, the city of nawabs and kebabs, has long been celebrated for its composite culture where Hindu and Muslim traditions blend seamlessly. Yet even this city of legendary tehzeeb (etiquette) and shared heritage had experienced moments of communal tension that tested the fabric of its pluralistic identity.

On a quiet street in Old Lucknow, I discovered a small Hanuman temple that at first glance seemed unremarkable—a modest structure with an orange flag fluttering above it, visited by a steady stream of devotees bringing flowers and offering prayers.

What caught my attention wasn't the temple itself but the person cleaning its floors early one morning—a Muslim man in a skullcap and kurta-pajama, meticulously sweeping the marble with careful, reverent movements.

The sight was unusual enough that I lingered, watching as he finished sweeping and began washing the floor with water mixed with rose essence, creating a fragrant welcome for the day's visitors. When he noticed my curious gaze, he smiled and greeted me with a gentle "*Adaab*," the traditional Muslim salutation.

His name was Rafiq Bhai, a tailor by profession who lived in the neighborhood. When I asked about his connection to the temple, his expression grew both solemn and warm.

"*Yeh mandir humne milkar banaya hai*" ~ "We built this temple together," he said, gesturing around with a sense of quiet pride.

The story he shared transported me back fifteen years, to a time when tensions between Hindu and Muslim communities had flared in parts of the city. During a brief but violent episode of rioting, the small temple that had stood at this spot for generations had been partially destroyed.

Rafiq's best friend since childhood was Ramesh, a Hindu whose family had been caretakers of the temple for three generations. The two men had grown up playing together, sharing meals in each other's homes, celebrating each other's festivals—a living example of Lucknow's syncretic traditions.

When the temple was damaged, Ramesh was heartbroken. Though no one in the immediate neighborhood had participated in the violence, the temple stood as a painful symbol of the division that had momentarily overcome their normally peaceful coexistence.

"*Ramesh ro raha tha, aur uska dard dekhkar mujhe bhi rona aa gaya*" ~ "Ramesh was crying, and seeing his pain made me cry too," Rafiq recalled. "*Maine kaha, 'Ro mat. Hum dono milkar ise phir se banayenge.'*" "I said, 'Don't cry. We will rebuild it together.'"

Against warnings from both communities that such an action might provoke further tension, the two friends began to clean up the debris. Gradually, others joined them—first a few neighbors, then more community members from both faiths. What started as a gesture of friendship became a collective act of healing.

"*Kisi ne cement laaya, kisi ne patthar, kisi ne apne haath ki mehnat di*" ~ "Someone brought cement, someone brought stones, someone contributed the labor of their hands," Rafiq explained. "*Mussalman bhi the, Hindu bhi. Sab ne kaam kiya.*" ~ "There were both Muslims and Hindus. Everyone worked."

The rebuilt temple, completed in just a few weeks, became stronger than before—not just physically but as a symbol of the community's resilience against forces that would divide them.

Since then, Rafiq had made it his personal duty to clean the temple once a week, a ritual of respect and a reaffirmation of the bonds that connected him to his Hindu neighbors. Ramesh did the same at the local mosque, though with less visible tasks since he could not enter certain areas as a non-Muslim.

"*Log aate hain aur dekhte hain—ek Mussalman mandir saaf kar raha hai. Unhein achha lagta hai*" ~ "People come and see—a

Muslim cleaning the temple. They feel good about it," he said. "*Bacchon ko bhi siksha milti hai ki dharm alag ho sakte hain, lekin insaniyat ek hai.*" "Children also learn that religions might be different, but humanity is one."

As worshippers began to arrive for morning prayers, Rafiq respectfully stepped aside, his task complete. Before leaving, he placed his hand on the temple wall for a moment—not in worship but in an unmistakable gesture of affection.

"*Insaaniyat sabse badi mazhab hai, sahab*" ~ "Humanity is the greatest religion, sir," he said as we parted ways, echoing the words I had heard from Pandit Hari Prasad in Hyderabad.

From two people of different faiths, in different cities, I had heard the same profound truth—suggesting that perhaps, beneath the visible diversity of India's religious expressions, runs a deeper current of shared values that unites more than divides.

Faith in Action: Small Moments, Great Meaning

Throughout my journey, I encountered countless other moments where faith revealed itself not in grand ceremonies or theological debates but in simple acts of kindness, courage, and connection:

The Millionaire Who Swept the Temple

At the Kapaleeshwarar Temple in Chennai, I noticed a man in a crisp white shirt and gold-rimmed glasses, sweeping the temple floors with deep concentration. His hands were soft, unused to physical labor, yet he cleaned with reverent focus.

Later, I learned he was one of the city's wealthiest real estate developers. Years ago, he had been a poor boy selling flowers outside this same temple.

"*Main yahan apni maa ke saath bheekh maangne aata tha. Aaj main yahan seva kar raha hoon*" ~ "I used to come here with my mother to beg. Today, I come here to serve," he explained.

His success had not made him forget his roots; instead, it had deepened his gratitude. Every week, he returned to sweep the floors of the temple that had witnessed his journey from destitution to abundance—a personal ritual of thanksgiving more meaningful to him than any offering of money.

The Beggar Who Could Not Stop Giving

Outside the Hanuman Mandir in Delhi's Connaught Place, I watched as a frail old man in tattered clothes stood in line to make an offering. When his turn came, he dropped a single one-rupee coin into the donation box—perhaps all he had.

When I asked him about it later, his response humbled me:

"*Beta, maine do din se kuch nahi khaya, lekin bhagwan ke saath samjhauta nahi kar sakta*" ~ "Son, I haven't eaten in two days, but I cannot compromise with God," he said.

His faith wasn't diminished by his poverty; in some ways, it seemed magnified by it. The rupee he gave represented a far greater proportion of his wealth than the hundreds left by more affluent devotees—a reminder of the true measure of generosity.

The Atheist Who Restored a Church

In Goa, I met a man supervising the renovation of a small Portuguese-era church. The quality of the work and his attention to historical detail impressed me, and I assumed he must be a devoted Christian.

"*Main bhagwan ko nahi maanta, par main insaaniyat ko maanta hoon*" ~ "I don't believe in God, but I believe in humanity," he told me when I asked about his faith.

The church had once sheltered his family during a devastating flood when he was a child. Decades later, when he heard the historic building was deteriorating due to lack of funds, he funded its restoration himself—not out of religious devotion but from gratitude for the sanctuary it had provided when he needed it most.

The True Measure of Faith

As my journey across India showed me the many faces of faith, I began to understand that its true measure lies not in theological knowledge, ritual precision, or religious identity, but in the simple question: What does your faith make you do?

Does it make you cross religious boundaries to help someone in need? Does it help you find strength when all external support has failed? Does it inspire you to rebuild what others have destroyed? Does it fill you with gratitude expressed through service? Does it open your hand to give even when you have almost nothing? Does it move you to honor debts of kindness regardless of who provided them?

In a country where religion is often a divisive force in politics and society, I found countless examples of faith as a unifying power in individual lives—instances where people's deepest beliefs, whether religious or secular, moved them toward greater compassion, courage, and connection.

The label mattered less than the action. The theology mattered less than the impact. Hindu, Muslim, Christian, atheist—the categories seemed to fade in importance when compared to the simple question of how faith manifested in a person's engagement with the world and with others.

Perhaps that is why the same phrase—"Humanity is the greatest religion"—echoed across different faiths and contexts throughout my journey. It wasn't a rejection of traditional religion but a recognition of its highest purpose: to make us more fully human, more deeply connected to one another, more capable of seeing beyond differences to our shared needs and hopes.

True faith, I learned, is not measured by how loudly it proclaims itself but by how quietly it transforms both the one who holds it and the world around them.

Chapter 11:
Conversations with Cab Drivers

Journeys Beyond Destinations

A cab ride is rarely just a journey from one place to another.

It's a temporary bubble in time and space—a strange intimacy between strangers who may never meet again. For fifteen minutes or an hour, two lives intersect in a moving metal box, creating a unique space for conversations that might never happen elsewhere.

In my corporate life, I had taken hundreds of cab rides. I'd sit in the back seat, absorbed in emails or phone calls, viewing the driver as nothing more than a necessary service provider—a human component of my transportation, less interesting than the smartphone in my hand.

But after selling my Mercedes and stepping into the real world, I began to see cab drivers differently. I started sitting in the front seat. I began asking questions. I listened to their stories.

And what stories they were!

The person behind the wheel might be a former business owner who lost everything overnight, an ex-soldier who faced death daily, a father working double shifts for his daughter's dreams, a widow defying social conventions, or an artist whose stage had become the driver's seat.

This chapter is about those unexpected conversations that turned ordinary rides into extraordinary journeys of understanding. It's about the wisdom found on winding roads, the confessions shared at traffic signals, and the life lessons learned while moving through the cities of India—one cab ride at a time.

The Fallen Entrepreneur — Mumbai

It was a rainy evening in Mumbai. The kind where the sky opens up without warning, turning streets into shallow rivers and bringing traffic to a near standstill. Water drummed on rooftops, pedestrians huddled under any available shelter, and wipers worked furiously against windshields in a losing battle against the downpour.

I had just finished meeting a friend in Bandra and needed to get back to my lodging in Dadar. After getting soaked despite my umbrella, I gratefully slid into a cab that had answered my frantic waving.

The driver, Raghav, was a man in his mid-50s with salt-and-pepper hair and a neatly trimmed mustache. Unlike most Mumbai cabbies who drove with a certain aggressive urgency, he navigated the chaotic traffic with unusual calmness, his movements unhurried despite the weather conditions.

"*Baarish mein traffic bahut bad hai. Time lagega pahunchne mein*" ~ "Traffic is very bad in the rain. It will take time to reach," he said in a measured tone, more as a statement of fact than an apology.

I nodded, settling in for what was clearly going to be a long ride. As we inched forward in the gridlock, I noticed how immaculately clean his cab was compared to most—no clutter on the dashboard, the seats well-maintained, even a subtle air freshener that managed to overcome the damp smell of rain.

"*Aap kitne saalon se gaadi chala rahe hain?*" ~ "How many years have you been driving?" I asked, making conversation.

He glanced at me in the rearview mirror. "*Sirf paanch saal.*" ~ "Just five years."

His answer surprised me. Most cabbies I'd met had been driving for decades, the profession often inherited by fathers or relatives. Five years suggested a late entry into the field.

"*Aur pehle kya karte the?*" ~ "And what did you do before this?" I asked, curious.

There was a pause, a slight tightening of his grip on the steering wheel.

"*Mere paas apni ek company thi*" ~ "I had my own company," he finally said quietly.

His unexpected answer shifted something in the atmosphere of the cab. As the rain continued to pour outside and we remained stuck in traffic, Raghav shared his story—not with self-pity but with the reflective clarity of someone who had processed a personal tragedy.

For nearly twenty years, he had run a successful textile export business, shipping fine garments to Europe and the Middle East. He showed me pictures on his phone of his former self—in a suit at international trade fairs, shaking hands with foreign buyers, and standing proudly in front of his factory.

"*Teen factories thi, 200 se zyada workers. Do ghar, teen gaadiyaan, foreign holidays har saal*" ~ "I had three factories, more than 200 workers. Two houses, three cars, foreign holidays every year)," he recounted, his voice matter of fact rather than boastful.

Then came a perfect storm of misfortune: a major European client defaulted on payment, a business partner embezzled funds, and the global economic downturn hit the export market. Within eighteen months, his business collapsed entirely.

"*Sirf ek saal laga sab kuch girne mein*" ~ "It took only one year for everything to collapse," he said, navigating around a large puddle with the same careful precision with which he told his story. "*Factories gayi, ghar gaya, bank balance khatam.*" ~ "The factories went, the house went, and the bank balance finished."

At forty-eight, with responsibilities to his family and no employment prospects, he had sold his last remaining asset—a luxury car—and used the money to buy this taxi.

"*Ghar chalana tha, toh gaadi chalani shuru kar di*" ~ "I had to run my home, so I started driving a car," he said with simple dignity.

As we finally broke free of the worst traffic and picked up speed, I asked him if he ever felt angry about his fate.

He thought for a moment, then replied: "*Zindagi ek pal mein badal sakti hai. Bas shikayat nahi karni chahiye.*" ~ "Life can change in a moment. You just shouldn't complain."

His lack of bitterness struck me deeply. Here was a man who had lost an empire yet spoke of it with philosophical acceptance rather than resentment. He had rebuilt his life from the wreckage of his dreams, finding dignity in work that society often looked down upon.

As we approached my destination, he mentioned that his son was now in college studying business administration.

"*Use kehta hoon—success milegi zaroor, par uski taarif nahi karni chahiye. Haar ka bhi samman karna chahiye*" ~ "I tell him—success will certainly come, but one shouldn't praise it too much. One should also respect defeat," he said as I paid the fare.

That rainy evening in Mumbai, I received more than just transportation. I got a masterclass in resilience, in accepting life's unpredictability with grace, and in the dignity of doing whatever work is necessary to meet one's responsibilities.

As I watched Raghav's taillights disappear into the rainy night, I realized that the man driving me might sometimes have more wisdom than the person being driven.

The Soldier Who Never Retired — Delhi

In Delhi, I hired a cab to take me from Connaught Place to the distant suburbs of Gurgaon. The moment I approached the vehicle, I sensed something different about both the car and its driver.

The cab was spotlessly clean, with not a speck of dust on the dashboard or seats despite Delhi's notorious pollution. The driver stood beside it with a straight posture that immediately suggested military training—shoulders back, chin up, an alertness in his bearing that stood out from the casual stance of most cabbies.

He was in his late forties, with close-cropped hair graying at the temples and a neatly trimmed mustache. He opened the door for me with a crisp "*Welcome, sir*" which further confirmed my impression.

As we navigated Delhi's chaotic traffic, his driving reflected the same disciplined approach— precise, cautious but confident, following rules that many others ignored. His cab moved through the anarchy of Delhi roads like an island of order in a sea of chaos.

"*Aap pehle fauj mein the kya?*" ~ "Were you in the army before?" I asked directly.

His eyes met mine in the rearview mirror, showing slight surprise at my observation.

"*Haan sir, 18 saal tak*" ~ "Yes sir, for 18 years," he replied with evident pride.

His name was Surinder Singh, and he had served in the Indian Army in some of the country's most challenging terrains—the high-altitude warfare of Siachen Glacier and the conflict zones of Kargil. For nearly two decades, he had lived a life where death was a daily possibility and extreme conditions were the norm.

"*Siachen mein temperature minus 50 degrees tak jaata hai, sir. Saas lete hi naak ke andar paani freeze ho jaata hai*" ~ "In Siachen, the temperature drops to minus 50 degrees, sir. The moment you breathe, the water inside your nose freezes," he explained, describing conditions most civilians could hardly imagine.

He spoke of friends lost to both enemy fire and the mountains themselves—soldiers who succumbed to avalanches, extreme cold, or the invisible killer of high-altitude pulmonary edema.

"*Zindagi ka asli rang wahan dikhta hai, jab maut roz saamne hoti hai*" ~ "The real colors of life appear when death is in front of you every day," he said thoughtfully.

Yet despite these challenges, there was a note of nostalgia in his voice when he spoke of his military service—a sense that those years, difficult as they were, had provided purpose, camaraderie, and a clear sense of identity.

The transition to civilian life had proven surprisingly challenging. After retirement, he discovered that his pension was inadequate for supporting his family in an expensive city like Delhi. More disheartening was how few employers valued his military experience.

"*Log kehte hain—army mein kya seekha? Computers nahi aate, marketing nahi aata*" ~ "People say—what did you learn in the army? You don't know computers, and you don't know marketing," he explained with a hint of frustration. "*Koi nahi poochta ki discipline kya hota hai, leadership kya hoti hai, pressure mein kaam karna kya hota hai.*" ~ "Nobody asks what discipline is or what leadership is, what working under pressure is."

Faced with limited options, he had invested his retirement benefits in buying a car and becoming a cab driver— a job that at least allowed him the independence he valued.

"*Ghar chalane ke liye socha, chalo taxi chalayenge*" ~ "To run my house, I thought, let's drive a taxi," he said matter-of-factly.

As our journey continued, I learned that many of his army colleagues had faced similar challenges after retirement—trained for warfare but unprepared for job markets, experts in survival but novices in self-promotion, heroes on the battlefield but anonymous in civilian streets.

When I asked if he regretted his military career given these difficulties, his reaction was immediate and firm.

"*Kabhi nahi, sir. Desh ke liye kaam karna sabse bada saubhagya hai*" ~ "Never, sir. Working for the country is the greatest fortune," he said, his spine straightening even more at the question. "*Har din miss karta hoon fauj ko. Lekin jeevan kisi bhi mode par rukna nahi chahiye.*" ~ "I miss the army every day. But life should not stop at any turn."

That last statement stayed with me long after our journey ended. Despite the lack of recognition for his service, despite the economic necessity that had put him behind the wheel of a cab, Surinder Singh maintained the uncompromising dignity and forward momentum of a soldier.

He had transferred his military values—duty, discipline, and excellence—to his civilian occupation, turning a humble cab into a space of order and professionalism. And in doing so, he reminded me that a uniform can be taken off, but the inner qualities it represents remain.

The Father Driving for His Daughter's Future — Chennai

In Chennai, I hired a cab for a day of sightseeing around the city's famous temples and beaches. My driver, Sundaram, was a cheerful, talkative man in his early fifties who insisted on playing Tamil film songs throughout our journey.

"*Old songs best songs, sir. New music, all computer, no feeling,*" he explained in his limited but expressive English, cranking up the volume on a melodious A.R. Rahman tune.

The music created a perfect backdrop to Chennai's colorful streets— the bright temple gopurams, the flower markets bursting with jasmine and marigold, the Marina Beach promenade lined with vendors and visitors. Sundaram provided enthusiastic commentary throughout, his love for his city evident in every explanation.

During lunch, I invited him to join me at a small restaurant, breaking the usual barrier between driver and passenger. As we shared a meal of dosas and filter coffee, our conversation deepened beyond tourist information to personal stories.

With visible pride, Sundaram pulled out his wallet to show me a photograph of a young woman in graduation attire, holding a certificate and smiling broadly.

"*My daughter, Meenakshi,*" he said, his face lighting up. "*First rank in college. Very brilliant girl.*"

As he spoke about Meenakshi, his entire demeanor changed. This wasn't just parental pride—it was something deeper, a profound investment in his daughter's future that gave meaning to his own life.

Meenakshi had completed her undergraduate degree in computer science with top honors and had recently been accepted to a master's program in the United States—an achievement that represented a quantum leap for a family where Sundaram himself had never finished high school.

"*America study is very costly, sir. But my daughter, she deserves a chance,*" he explained.

To fund her education, Sundaram had been working double shifts for the past two years—driving his regular hours for the cab company, then taking private bookings during his off-hours. He had sold family land, taken loans, and saved every extra rupee.

"*I wake up at 4:30 in the morning. Sleep at 12:30 at night. Seven days working, no holiday,*" he said matter-of-factly, without a hint of complaint in his voice.

What struck me most was his acceptance—even embrace—of the fact that his daughter's success would take her far from him, perhaps permanently. Unlike many Indian parents who expected their children to remain close and care for them in old age, Sundaram spoke of Meenakshi's likely future in America with unalloyed joy.

"*Sir, village bird make nests teach baby flying, then baby go away. This natural life,*" he said with simple wisdom. "*My father never left village. I never leave Tamil Nadu. My daughter will see the world.*"

The sacrifice was not just financial but deeply emotional. He was working exhausting hours to fund a future that would likely separate him from the person he loved most, in a country where family bonds are traditionally maintained through physical proximity.

"*Main jaanta hoon ek din meri beti mujhe chhodegi. Par main usko uda dekhna chahta hoon*" ~ "I know one day my daughter will leave me. But I want to see her fly," he said, switching to Hindi when his English couldn't fully express his feelings.

When I asked if he would miss her, his eyes grew momentarily misty. "*Missing is a small price, sir. Her success is a big reward.*"

As we continued our tour of Chennai that afternoon, I saw the city differently—not just through the eyes of a proud local showing a visitor around, but through the perspective of a father whose daily labor on these streets was paving a path for his daughter to transcend them.

Sundaram's story embodied one of the most powerful and poignant aspects of parental love—the willingness to sacrifice not just for a child's happiness but for their independence, even when that independence might create distance.

His cab wasn't just a vehicle for tourists; it was the launch pad for a daughter's dreams. And in his humble determination to give Meenakshi wings, I witnessed a form of love both selfless and profound.

The Widow Who Conquered Fear — Bengaluru

In Bengaluru, India's Silicon Valley, I had an experience that challenged my preconceptions from the moment I booked the cab.

When the car arrived, I was surprised to see a woman in a maroon saree behind the wheel. Female cab drivers are still rare in India, where driving professionally remains a predominantly male occupation fraught with safety concerns for women.

The driver introduced herself as Lakshmi, a woman in her early forties with a quiet confidence and hands that gripped the wheel with assurance. She wore simple gold bangles, a small bindi on her forehead, and dark sunglasses that she kept on even as evening approached.

As we drove through Bengaluru's notorious traffic, I noticed how skillfully she handled the car—neither timid nor aggressive, but measured and confident. She navigated the chaos with a calm efficiency that many male drivers lacked.

"*Aapko driving kab se aati hai?*" ~ "How long have you known how to drive?" I asked.

"*Sirf teen saal. Pehle kabhi zaroorat nahi padi*" ~ "Only three years. Before that, I never needed to," she replied.

Her answer surprised me. Most professional drivers had been driving since their teens. I asked what had changed three years ago.

There was a momentary silence, then: "*Teen saal pehle mera pati accident mein chala gaya.*" ~ "Three years ago, my husband died in an accident."

The simple sentence contained volumes of unspoken grief. Lakshmi had been a homemaker for twenty years, raising two children while her husband worked as an accountant. His sudden death had left her without financial support and with teenage children still in school.

"*Mere paas koi skill nahi thi, sir. Na degree, na experience*" ~ "I had no skills, sir. No degree, no experience," she explained. "*Log kehte the—kisi ke ghar kaam kar lo, ya phir kapde silna seekh lo.*" ~ "People said— work as a housemaid or learn to stitch clothes."

But Lakshmi had different ideas. Her husband had taught her to drive their family car, though she rarely took the wheel while he was alive. After his death, she decided to use this skill to support her family—a choice that met with strong disapproval from relatives and neighbors.

"*Mujhe log aksar puchte hain, tumhe dar nahi lagta?*" ~ "People often ask me, aren't you scared?" she said, navigating around a bus with practiced ease. "*Main kehti hoon, dar unko lagta hai jo haar maan lete hain.*" ~ "I tell them, only those who give up feel fear."

Her journey to becoming a cab driver had not been easy. She had to overcome not only her own initial fears but also active resistance from others. Male drivers at the taxi stand harassed her. Relatives stopped speaking to her. Some passengers refused to ride with a female driver or made inappropriate comments.

"*Pehle hafta roz roti thi ghar jakar*" ~ "The first week, I would cry every day after going home," she admitted. "*Phir socha—mere aansu mere bacchon ka pet nahi bharenge.*" ~ "Then I thought—my tears wouldn't fill my children's stomachs."

So she persisted. Each day became slightly easier than the last. She learned to handle difficult situations, developed a thicker skin against comments, and gradually earned respect from fellow drivers and regular customers.

Now, three years later, she owned her car instead of renting it, had regular clients who specifically requested her, and had built a reputation for reliability and safety that kept her schedule full.

"*Mere bete ne engineering start kiya hai. Beti medical ki taiyari kar rahi hai*" ~ "My son has started engineering. My daughter is preparing for medical entrance," she said with quiet pride. "*Unke liye main kuch bhi kar sakti hoon.*" ~ "I can do anything for them."

When I asked about the sunglasses she wore even as darkness fell, she hesitated, then removed them briefly. A faded scar ran from her eyebrow to her cheekbone—a reminder of domestic violence she had endured silently during her marriage.

"*Kabhi kabhi, jo cheez humein tod sakti hai, wahi humein mazboot bana deti hai*" ~ "Sometimes, the thing that can break us makes us stronger," she said quietly as she put the glasses back on. "*Mujhe aadat hai mushkilon se ladne ki.*" ~ "I am accustomed to fighting difficulties."

As we reached my destination and I prepared to leave her cab, Lakshmi shared a final thought: "*Aurat ki sabse badi taakat hai uska azaad hona. Main apne bacchon ko yehi sikha rahi hoon.*" ~ "A woman's greatest strength is her independence. This is what I'm teaching my children."

In Bengaluru's sea of male cab drivers, Lakshmi had carved out her own space—transforming tragedy into opportunity, societal disapproval into determination, and fear into courage. Her story was not just about economic survival but about reclaiming agency in a society that often denies it to women, especially widows.

As her cab disappeared into the evening traffic, I thought about how each journey with her was not just a ride but a small act of revolution against limiting expectations.

The Singer Behind the Wheel — Kolkata

Kolkata, with its deep cultural roots and artistic heritage, gave me perhaps the most unexpected cab experience of all.

It was a rainy evening when I hailed a yellow Ambassador cab—those iconic, bulbous vehicles that still dominate Kolkata's streets long after they've disappeared from most other Indian cities. As I settled into the worn leather seat and gave my destination, the driver—a man in his sixties with kind eyes and a face etched with experience—nodded and pulled into traffic.

We had traveled only a few blocks when he began to sing.

His voice was extraordinary—rich, melodious, and trained in the classical tradition. The Bengali song he sang had a melancholy beauty that filled the cab's interior, somehow blending perfectly with the rhythmic swish of wipers against the windshield and the patter of rain on the roof.

I sat transfixed, not understanding the words but feeling their emotional impact. When he finished, the silence seemed almost intrusive.

"*Aapki awaaz bahut khoobsurat hai*" ~ "Your voice is very beautiful," I said.

He glanced at me in the rearview mirror and smiled slightly. "*Bachpan se shauk tha, lekin zindagi ne gaana chodwa diya*" ~ "I loved singing since childhood, but life forced me to stop," he replied.

His name was Ashok, and in his youth, he had been a promising vocalist, trained in Rabindra Sangeet—the songs composed by Nobel laureate Rabindranath Tagore that form an integral part of Bengali cultural identity. He had performed on local radio, at cultural events, and had even been offered opportunities to record.

Then his father fell ill, requiring expensive treatments that drained the family's modest savings. As the eldest son, Ashok had to set aside his artistic pursuits to support his parents and younger siblings.

"*Aaj bhi kabhi kabhi sochta hoon, agar sab theek rehta, toh main kisi aur jagah hota*" ~ "Sometimes I wonder, if things had gone right, I would have been somewhere else," he said, navigating through Kolkata's narrow streets with the ease of someone who had driven them for decades.

But unlike many stories of abandoned dreams, Ashok's didn't end in bitterness. Though he never became the professional singer he had hoped to be, he had found ways to keep music in his life. He sang at community gatherings, taught vocal lessons to neighborhood children for free, and—most touchingly—turned his cab into a mobile concert hall, singing for passengers who seemed receptive.

"*Dukh toh hai, par agar zindagi nahi mili jo maangi thi, toh jo mili hai usko accha bana dete hain,*" (Yes, I feel sad. But if I didn't get the life I asked for, I will make the life I got beautiful) he explained with a philosopher's resignation.

As we continued through rain-slicked streets, he sang another song at my request— this one more upbeat, his fingers tapping a rhythm on the steering wheel at stop lights. For those moments, the cab was transformed. He was no longer just a driver, and I no longer just a passenger. We were audience and performer, connected by the universal language of music.

When we reached my destination, I asked if he ever regretted not pursuing his singing career more determinedly.

He thought for a moment before answering: "*Mere papa ke liye kiya tha. Unka ilaaj, unki dekhbhal—yeh bhi ek tareeke se gaana hi tha. Bass raag alag tha.*" ~ "I did it for my father. His treatment, his care—this too was a kind of song. Just a different raga."

The wisdom in his response struck me deeply. He had reframed his sacrifice not as an abandonment of his dream but as a different expression of his art—the art of devotion, of duty, of love.

As I paid the fare and prepared to step out into the rain, he said something I will never forget: "*Zindagi mein kabhi koi sangeet khatam nahi hota. Bass kabhi dhima ho jata hai, kabhi tez. Hume bas sunna seekhna chahiye.*" ~ "In life, no music ever really ends. It just becomes softer sometimes, louder other times. We just need to learn how to listen."

I stood in the rain watching his cab disappear into the Kolkata traffic, carrying with it a voice that deserved concert halls but had found its stage behind a steering wheel instead.

The Person Behind the Wheel

My journey across India brought me face to face with dozens of cab drivers—each with a unique story that challenged my assumptions and expanded my understanding.

I met:

- A former business tycoon who had lost everything but maintained his dignity
- An ex-soldier who transferred his military discipline to civilian roads
- A devoted father working impossible hours for his daughter's future

- A widowed woman who defied society's expectations to support her family
- A gifted singer who found a way to keep his music alive despite life's demands

Their stories reminded me that the person driving the vehicle is often more extraordinary than the passenger being driven. Behind the wheel might sit a philosopher, an artist, a hero, or a quiet revolutionary—someone whose journey through life offers wisdom that no travel destination can match.

When we enter a cab, we're not just purchasing transportation; we're briefly intersecting with another life, another set of dreams, struggles, and triumphs. The real journey happens not on the road but in the exchange of stories, in the momentary connection between strangers who would otherwise never meet.

Now, whenever I take a cab, I sit in the front seat. I ask questions. I listen. Because I've learned that sometimes, the most important destination isn't the address you give when you enter—it's the understanding you take with you when you leave.

Chapter 12:
The Good, The Bad, and The Grey

Between Black and White

Life is rarely pure black or pure white.

Most of us exist in the vast expanse of grey between absolute goodness and absolute evil. We make choices—some selfless, some selfish, some a complex mixture of both—shaped by our circumstances, our struggles, and the hand we've been dealt.

Before I sold my Mercedes, I had a simpler view of the world. People seemed easier to categorize: the successful and the struggling, the educated and the illiterate, the law-abiding and the criminal. But as I traveled across India by bus and train, walking streets I would have previously only seen through tinted windows, I discovered that human complexity defies such easy labels.

I met people who did extraordinary good despite crushing hardships. I encountered individuals whose lives appeared morally questionable yet who showed remarkable kindness. I witnessed how circumstances could push good people toward bad choices—and how sometimes, within those seemingly bad choices, a profound goodness could emerge.

This chapter is about those grey areas—about people whose lives challenge our preconceptions, whose choices defy simple judgment, and whose stories remind us that true character isn't about moral perfection but about how we respond to the circumstances life has given us.

The Teacher Who Sold Vegetables — Jaipur

It was a warm evening in Jaipur. The pink sandstone buildings glowed orange in the setting sun, and the streets were filled with people heading home after work or shopping for dinner ingredients.

Near my guesthouse, I stopped at a small vegetable stall to buy some fruit. The vendor was a middle-aged man with graying hair at his temples and wire-rimmed glasses that gave him a scholarly appearance. Unlike other vendors who called out to passersby, he arranged his produce with quiet precision, his movements methodical and deliberate.

When I approached to buy some bananas, I was struck by how differently he spoke compared to typical street vendors. His Hindi was formal and articulate, his manner polite but reserved.

"*Kitni chaahiye?*" ~ "How many would you like?" he asked, his pronunciation clear and refined.

As he weighed the fruit on his old-fashioned brass scale, I noticed calluses on his hands—but they weren't the weathered hands of someone who had spent a lifetime in physical labor. They seemed newer, as if the work was not his lifelong profession.

Intrigued, I struck up a conversation, asking how business was going.

"*Acha chal raha hai. Logon ko sabzi toh roz hi chaahiye*" ~ "It's going well. People need vegetables every day" he replied with a small smile that didn't quite reach his eyes.

There was something about his demeanor—a dignity, an attentiveness, a particular way of explaining the quality of different vegetables—that seemed out of place in a roadside stall. When a young boy passed by and respectfully greeted him as "*Gupta sir*," my curiosity peaked.

"*Aap teacher hain?*" ~ "Are you a teacher?" I asked directly.

He looked up, momentarily surprised, then nodded.

"*Haan. Din mein school mein padhaata hoon. Shaam ko yeh kaam karta hoon*" ~ "Yes. During the day I teach in a school. In the evening I do this work," he admitted.

His name was Vikram Gupta, and he had been a history teacher at a respected government school for over twenty years. By day, he educated hundreds of students about India's past; by evening, he sold vegetables from this small cart.

"*Sirf raat ko yeh kaam karta hoon. Din mein school mein padhaata hoon*" ~ "I do this only at night. During the day, I teach in school," he explained, adjusting his glasses in a professorial gesture that seemed incongruous behind a vegetable stall.

I asked what had driven him to take on this second job, expecting perhaps a story of debt or financial hardship.

He glanced at a worn photograph pinned to the underside of his cart's umbrella—a young woman in graduation attire, smiling proudly. His daughter.

"*Meri beti ko doctor banana hai. Uske sapne chhote nahi hain, toh mera mehnat bhi chhota nahi ho sakta*" ~ "My daughter wants to be a doctor. Her dreams aren't small, so my efforts can't be small either," he said, his voice softening with pride.

The economics were simple but brutal. His teacher's salary was respectable but insufficient for the staggering costs of private medical college. Rather than tell his daughter to aim lower, he had chosen to supplement his income—taking on this second job that he kept hidden from his colleagues at school.

"*Log kya kahenge—master ji sabzi bech rahe hain?*" ~ "What would people say—a teacher selling vegetables?" he said with a wry smile. "*Par kuch cheezein izzat se badhkar hoti hain.*" ~ "But some things are more important than pride."

He had been doing this for three years, working twelve-hour days between teaching and selling vegetables. His wife helped with the procurement from wholesale markets early in the morning, while he handled evening sales after school hours.

"*Bas do saal aur. Phir meri beti doctor ban jayegi, aur main phir se sirf teacher ho jaunga*" ~ "Just two more years. Then my daughter will become a doctor, and I will go back to being just a teacher," he said.

What struck me most was not the sacrifice itself—parents around the world make tremendous sacrifices for their children—but the grace with which he carried it. There was no resentment, no self-pity, just a quiet determination to give his daughter opportunities he never had.

As I paid for my fruit, I watched him adjust his glasses and begin meticulously reorganizing his display for the evening rush. In that moment, he was both a humble vegetable seller and a dignified educator—a man living in the grey area between social expectations and parental love, choosing the latter regardless of how others might judge him.

The Woman Who Fought Trafficking — Mumbai

In Mumbai's red-light district of Kamathipura, life exists in raw, unfiltered form. Narrow lanes lined with small rooms, women sitting on plastic chairs outside, calling to passing men, pimps negotiating prices in hushed tones—it's a world most of us glimpse only in news reports or films, if at all.

I had come here with a social worker who was introducing me to various community initiatives in Mumbai. As we walked through the area in the early evening, the atmosphere was both electric and oppressive—neon signs flickering to life, the scent of cheap perfume mingling with cooking spices from tiny kitchens, music blaring from different directions, creating a discordant symphony.

In a small room converted into a makeshift office, I met Lakshmi, a woman in her mid-thirties with striking eyes that held both weariness and determination. She was a commercial sex worker—not by choice, but by circumstance, having been trafficked from Nepal as a teenager.

But what made her extraordinary wasn't her past; it was what she did with her present.

"*Mujhe yeh kaam pasand nahi. Par jab tak mujhe karna pad raha hai, tab tak kisi aur ko ismein ghusne se bachana hai*" ~ "I don't like this work. But as long as I have to do it, I must stop others from being forced into it," she told me, her voice low but steady.

For the past five years, Lakshmi had been using a significant portion of her earnings to fund a small shelter for girls rescued from trafficking. The shelter, run from a rented apartment a few blocks away, currently housed seven girls between the ages of 13 and 17—all of whom had been intercepted before being sold into the trade.

"*Har mahine meri kamayi ka aadha hissa un ladkiyon ke liye jata hai—unki padhai, khana, rehne ka kharcha*" ~ "Every month, half of my earnings go toward those girls—their education, food, housing expenses," she explained.

Her own life was constrained by the very system she fought against. Debt bondage, physical threats, and lack of alternative skills kept her trapped in sex work. Yet within those constraints, she had found a way to create profound positive change.

With the help of a sympathetic NGO worker, she had developed an informal network that identified vulnerable girls being brought into the city. Sometimes they could alert police to intercept traffickers; other times, they had to purchase the girls' freedom with their own money before they were forced into sex work.

"*Kabhi kabhi lagta hai ki main ek haath se zanjeer tod rahi hoon, aur dusre haath se khud zanjeer mein bandhi hoon*" ~ "Sometimes it feels like I'm breaking chains with one hand while being chained with the other," she said, capturing the contradiction of her existence.

What truly moved me was how she spoke about the girls in her shelter: not as victims to be pitied but as daughters to be guided toward a better future. She insisted they attend school, learn vocational skills, and build the confidence they would need to live independently.

"*Main unhe dikhana chahti hoon ki aurat ke paas choice hoti hai, power hoti hai—chahe woh kitni bhi garib ho*" ~ "I want to show them that a woman has choices, has power—no matter how poor she is," she said, her eyes flashing with conviction.

In a social system that often views sex workers as either criminals or helpless victims with no moral agency, Lakshmi defied categorization. Her life existed in a morally complex space—participating in a trade many consider immoral while simultaneously fighting against its worst abuses with remarkable courage.

As we left her small office, she returned to work—back to a reality I could scarcely imagine. But she had shown me that even in the darkest circumstances, the human capacity for compassion and resistance remains. Her life might have been forced into shadows, but the light she created for others was undeniable.

The Man Who Created Family from Nothing — Kolkata

At a small tea stall near College Street in Kolkata, amid the historic coffee houses and bookshops that have nurtured Bengali intellectuals for generations, I met an elderly man whose simple appearance belied an extraordinary story.

Binod-da, as everyone called him, was in his seventies, with a thin frame, white hair, and hands that trembled slightly as he sipped his tea. He wore a faded but clean dhoti and kurta, and spoke with the gentle lilt characteristic of Bengali elders.

The tea stall owner treated him with unusual respect, refusing payment and insisting on serving him personally. When I asked why, he simply said, "*Binod-da manush ke bachaata hai.*" ~ "Binod-da saves people."

Intrigued, I moved to Binod-da's table and introduced myself. He welcomed me with a warm smile and offered to share the plate of biscuits the shop owner had given him.

As our conversation unfolded, I learned that Binod-da had been an **orphan**, abandoned as an infant and raised in a government orphanage until age 18, when he was thrust into the world with minimal education and no family connections.

"*Mere paas kuch nahi tha—na maa-baap, na rishtedaar, na property*" ~ "I had nothing—no parents, no relatives, no property," he explained, his voice matter of fact rather than seeking sympathy. "*Sirf ek hi cheez thi—akelapan.*" ~ "Just one thing—loneliness."

He had managed to find work as a clerk in a small office, living frugally in a tiny, rented room. His life continued this way for years— simple, solitary, survival-focused—until one rainy evening when he found a child sleeping in the doorway of his building.

The boy, no more than five years old, had been abandoned by his mother who could no longer feed him. Rather than calling authorities, Binod-da made a decision that would change both their lives: he brought the child into his room, shared his meager dinner, and created space in his tiny life for another human being.

"*Pehli baar kisi ne mujhe 'baba' bulaya*" ~ "For the first time, someone called me 'father'," he recalled, his eyes glistening. "*Us din se zindagi badal gayi.*" ~ "From that day, life changed."

That first child, now a grown man working as a schoolteacher, became the beginning of what would evolve into Binod-da's unique mission. Over the next forty years, he would take in 27 abandoned children—never through formal adoption, but through a personal commitment to provide what he himself had never had: a sense of belonging.

He never married and lived his entire life in the same modest neighborhood, gradually moving to slightly larger accommodation as his unorthodox family grew. With no wealth or resources beyond his clerk's salary, he managed through frugality, community support, and sheer determination.

"*Main akela paida hua tha, akela marna nahi chahta*" ~ "I was born alone. I don't want to die alone," he said with disarming simplicity.

Today, his "children" include doctors, teachers, shopkeepers, and tradespeople—all of whom still visit him regularly, care for his needs in old age, and bring their own children to meet the man who saved them from abandonment.

When I asked what motivated him to take on such responsibility despite his limited means, he looked genuinely puzzled by the question.

"*Koi bhi insaan akela nahi reh sakta. Family chahiye—chahe woh khoon ki ho ya mohabbat ki*" ~ "No person can live alone. Everyone needs family— whether it's made from blood or from love," he said, as if stating an obvious truth.

Binod-da's life existed in the grey areas of social norms. He had never been a "proper" father in the eyes of the law. He had bent rules to help children without going through official channels. His methods would fail many institutional standards of child welfare.

Yet the results spoke for themselves—dozens of lives redirected from abandonment toward opportunity, and a man who had transformed his own orphaned emptiness into a rich tapestry of human connection.

As we finished our tea, several young people stopped by, greeting him with obvious affection, checking if he needed anything, sharing news of their lives. I watched as his face lit up with each interaction, and I understood: he hadn't just saved these children. In creating a family from nothing, he had also saved himself.

The Boy Who Worked for His Abuser — Varanasi

The ghats of Varanasi at sunset create one of India's most iconic images—stone steps descending to the sacred Ganges, lined with ancient temples, filled with pilgrims performing rituals, holy men in meditation, tourists capturing photographs, and locals going about their daily business.

Near Dashashwamedh Ghat, the city's main riverfront area, I noticed a young boy of perhaps 13 or 14 performing a fire dance for a small crowd of tourists. His movements were skillful and dramatic as he manipulated flaming torches, his thin body twisting and turning with remarkable control. After his performance, he collected money in a small cloth bag, counting it quickly before moving to another spot.

Something about his demeanor caught my attention—an intensity behind his showmanship, a certain gravity unusual in someone so young. I approached him during a break between performances, complimenting his skills. His name was Rohan, and he had been performing on the ghats for three years.

When I asked how he had learned such impressive fire manipulation, his answer took me by surprise: "*Necessity teaches you many skills, sir.*"

His mature response prompted me to invite him for a lassi at a nearby stall. Initially hesitant, he eventually agreed after assuring himself he could still fit in two more performances before night fell completely.

Over sweet lassi served in clay cups, Rohan gradually shared his story. He lived with his father in a small room in the maze-like alleys behind the ghats. His mother had left years ago, unable to endure his father's alcoholism and violent behavior.

"*Mere papa sharab pite hain. Bahut zyada*" ~ "My father drinks alcohol. Too much," he said, his eyes downcast. "*Jab woh pite hain, tab woh badal jate hain. Bahut maarte hain.*" ~ "When he drinks, he changes. He beats a lot."

The abuse had been constant for as long as Rohan could remember—drunken rages that left him bruised and terrified, nights spent hiding on rooftops to escape his father's violence, days of hunger when alcohol consumed the family's meager resources.

As he spoke, I struggled to understand why he hadn't run away, why he remained with someone who caused him such pain. Then came the revelation that shifted everything about his story.

Six months earlier, his father had collapsed in the middle of a drinking binge. The diagnosis was liver cirrhosis—advanced and life-threatening. Treatment would require expensive medication, diet changes, and eventually possible surgery—all far beyond the means of a drunk laborer and his son.

Rather than seeing this as an opportunity for escape, Rohan had doubled down on his street performances, adding the more dangerous fire dancing to his repertoire to earn more money. Every rupee not needed for absolute necessities went toward his father's treatment.

"*Aap itna kyun kar rahe ho? Unhone toh aapko sirf dukh diya hai*" ~ "Why are you doing so much? He has only given you pain" I asked, struggling to comprehend such devotion to an abuser.

Rohan looked at me directly, his young face showing wisdom far beyond his years.

"*Woh galat insaan hai, par mera pita toh hai,*" ~ "He is a bad person, but he is still my father," he said simply.

This wasn't a statement of resignation or blind loyalty. It carried a profound understanding of human complexity—that people can be both terribly flawed and still worthy of compassion, that relationships transcend simple categories of good and bad.

"*Jab woh nahi peete, tab unke andar achhai bhi hai*" ~ "When he's not drinking, there is goodness in him too," Rohan added. "*Bachpan mein kahaniyan sunate the, likhna-padhna sikhaya. Usi se aaj main zinda hoon.*" ~ "In my childhood, he would tell storiesand teach me to read and write. That's why I'm surviving today."

As the evening deepened and Rohan prepared for his final performance, he shared that his father had been sober for three weeks now—his longest stretch in years. The illness had become a painful but effective wake-up call.

"*Pata nahi kal kya hoga. Shaayad woh phir se peena shuru kar dein, shaayad badal jayein*" ~ "Don't know what will happen tomorrow. Maybe he'll start drinking again, maybe he'll change," Rohan said with a shrug that carried both hope and resignation.

Then he added: "*Par mujhe khud ko dekhna hai roz. Kya main sahi insaan ban raha hoon ya galat?*" ~ "But I need to look at myself every day. Am I becoming a good person or a bad one?"

As I watched him perform his final fire dance of the evening, his face illuminated by the flames he so skillfully controlled, I saw in this child both the victim of terrible circumstances and the hero of his own morally complex story—choosing compassion where hatred would have been justified, finding within himself the capacity for forgiveness that most adults struggle to achieve.

His life existed in the grey area where love and pain intertwine, where obligation meets choice, where the definitions of right and wrong blur into something more nuanced and human than any moral absolute could capture.

Brief Glimpses of Complex Humanity

As my journey continued, I collected other stories that existed in the morally complex middle ground—brief encounters that challenged simple judgments:

The Transgender Woman at the Temple

In Chennai, I met a transgender woman named Maya who had been rejected by her family but found purpose as a helper at a local temple. Though initially viewed with suspicion by conservative devotees, her dedication to keeping the temple grounds immaculate eventually won their respect.

"*Logon ne mujhe bahar nikala, par bhagwan ne andar bulaya*" ~ "People threw me out, but God called me in," she told me as she carefully arranged flowers for the deity. Her faith had given her dignity when society denied it, and in turn, her presence at the temple was slowly changing attitudes toward her community.

The Homeless Man's Meal

In Hyderabad, I witnessed a homeless man named Feroz share his only meal of the day with a stray dog. When I commented on his generosity despite his own hunger, he looked surprised.

"*Bhook toh sab ko lagti hai, insaan ho ya janwar*" ~ "Everyone feels hunger, whether human or animal," he said. "*Aur khana baantne se kam nahi hota, badhta hai.*" ~ "And food doesn't decrease by sharing; it increases."

In his destitution, he had maintained compassion and generosity that many with abundance struggle to achieve.

The Moral Landscape of Real Lives

As I reflect on these stories—the teacher selling vegetables, the sex worker saving girls, the orphan creating family, the boy caring for his abusive father—I'm struck by how poorly our usual moral categories serve to capture the rich complexity of actual human lives.

We live in a world that craves simple narratives—heroes and villains, saints and sinners, right and wrong. But the truth of human experience resists such neat classifications. Most of us exist in the vast middle ground—making the best choices we can with the limited options life has given us, carrying both light and shadow within our hearts, capable of both selfishness and profound sacrifice.

What seems to matter most is not moral perfection but moral direction—not whether we exist in the grey areas, but how we navigate them. Do we use our circumstances as excuses for cruelty, or do we find ways to express kindness despite them? Do we resign ourselves to our limitations, or do we strive to transcend them?

The most inspiring people I met weren't those who had lived perfect lives, but those who had chosen to move toward greater compassion, greater responsibility, and greater humanity—regardless of where they started from or what obstacles they faced.

Perhaps true character isn't revealed in the absence of moral challenges but in how we respond to them—in the teacher who sets aside pride for his daughter's future, in the sex worker who fights the system that exploits her, in the orphan who creates what he never had, in the boy who offers forgiveness when resentment would be easier.

Their lives remind us that goodness isn't about purity; it's about choice. It's about the direction we move in the vast grey landscape of human experience—step by imperfect step, toward the better angels of our nature.

Chapter 12.1: A Visit to the Kids' Cricket Coaching Academy

Dreams in the Himalayan Foothills

Some journeys are carefully planned. Others happen by beautiful accident.

The most meaningful experiences often come when we least expect them, when we step off our charted path and follow an unexpected trail of curiosity.

My visit to a hidden cricket academy in Dharamshala was one such serendipitous detour—a chance encounter that reminded me why travel without rigid itineraries can open doors to the most authentic human connections.

A Chain of Coincidences

I had come to Dharamshala with no specific agenda. After the intensity of India's major cities, I craved the tranquility of mountains, the simplicity of small-town life, and air untainted by urban pollution.

The morning was perfect— crisp Himalayan air filled my lungs as I stepped out of my modest guesthouse. The sky was impossibly blue, a shade that seemed to exist only at this altitude. The scent of pine trees drifted on the gentle breeze, and distant snow-capped peaks created a breathtaking backdrop to the town's simple buildings.

I stopped at a roadside chai stall near the bus stand, ordering a cup of masala chai and settled on a wooden bench to watch the unhurried rhythm of mountain life unfold. The vendor, an elderly man with deep smile lines around his eyes, noticed my relaxed demeanor.

"*Tourist ho?*" ~ "Are you a tourist?" he asked, expertly pouring tea from pot to glass, creating the perfect froth.

I explained that I was traveling across India, trying to experience the country beyond tourist sites and luxury hotels.

His eyes lit up as he handed me the steaming chai. "*Phir toh aapko hamare bacchon ko khelna dekhna chahiye*" ~ "Then you should see our children play," he said with unexpected enthusiasm. "*Idhar ke bacchon ko dekho, toh lagega jaise har koi Tendulkar banna chahta hai!*" ~ "If you see the kids here, you'll think each of them wants to become the next Tendulkar!"

Cricket, of course, was nothing unusual in India—a nation where the sport is less a game and more a religion. But something in the vendor's tone—a mixture of community pride and genuine excitement—caught my attention.

Later that day, while chatting with my hotel manager about hiking trails, I mentioned the chai vendor's comment about local cricket players.

"*Ah, woh academy ki baat kar rahe honge*" ~ "Ah, he must be talking about the academy," the manager nodded with recognition. "*Coach Anil ne pichle 15 saal se chalaya hai. Bahut talented bachche hain wahaan.*" ~ "Coach Anil has been running it for 15 years. There are very talented children there."

He proceeded to give me directions to a place where few tourists ever discovered—a small cricket academy tucked away near the hills, where local children trained with minimal resources but maximum heart.

"*Saab, ek baar jaake dekhiye. Jo junoon unmein hai, bade shehron ke stadiums mein bhi mushkil se dikhta hai*" ~ "Sir, go see them once. The passion they have—you won't even find it in the biggest stadiums," he suggested.

Something about his description intrigued me. The next morning, as the Himalayan mist still hung low over the valleys, I found myself walking along a dirt path, following hand-drawn directions to a destination that wasn't on any tourist map.

First Sight of the Field of Dreams

After a twenty-minute walk that took me away from the main town and toward more rural surroundings, I heard it before I saw it— the distinctive sound of leather hitting willow, followed by cheers and shouts in Hindi and the local Pahari dialect.

Rounding a bend in the path, I came upon a sight that stopped me in my tracks: a simple, rugged cricket ground carved out of the mountainside, with spectacular views of the Dhauladhar range in the background.

This was no manicured professional field. The pitch was hard-packed earth rather than carefully maintained grass. The boundaries were marked with stones rather than painted lines. A few practice nets stood at one end—weathered but functional. There was no pavilion, no electronic scoreboard, no floodlights—just a natural amphitheater where mountains met sport in its purest form.

But what truly captured my attention were the children. About twenty of them, ranging from perhaps eight to sixteen years old, were engaged in an intense practice session. Their appearance created an immediate contrast with the polished cricket academies I had glimpsed in bigger cities.

Many were barefoot, their feet toughened by regular practice without shoes. Others wore worn-out cricket shoes clearly handed down through multiple owners. Their jerseys were oversized, often bearing the names of professional players, but faded from countless washes. Some used professional cricket gear while others made do with makeshift equipment—pads crafted from repurposed materials, homemade batting gloves.

Yet the limitations of their equipment stood in stark contrast to the unlimited passion in their eyes. Each child moved with the focus and intensity of someone practicing for a world championship. Bowlers analyzed their deliveries with professional seriousness. Batsmen studied their technique after each shot. Fielders dived for catches with complete disregard for the hardness of the ground.

The sensory experience was captivating. The rhythmic thwack of bat meeting ball echoed against the mountains. The pounding of running feet on hard earth created a percussion backdrop. The calls between players—encouragement, instruction, celebration—formed a soundtrack to their practice. And everywhere I looked, I saw focused gazes that spoke of dreams far bigger than this humble field.

I stood watching from the periphery, reluctant to intrude on their practice but mesmerized by the scene before me. The children were so absorbed in their game that my presence went largely unnoticed.

The Man Behind the Academy

After about fifteen minutes, I became aware of someone watching me. A man—probably in his late 40s—stood a few yards away, observing my observation with curious but friendly eyes.

He approached with a confident stride, extending his hand in greeting. "*Namaskar. Main Anil hoon. Academy ke coach.*" ~ "Greetings. I'm Anil. The academy's coach."

Coach Anil had the weathered look of someone who spent most of his time outdoors. His skin was darkened by the sun, and his hands bore the calluses of someone who demonstrated cricket techniques daily. Despite his simple clothing— a tracksuit that had seen better days and a faded cricket cap— he carried himself with the quiet authority of someone who commanded respect without demanding it.

When I explained my journey and how I'd heard about the academy, his face broke into a warm smile.

"*Toh aap hamare chote se cricket academy mein kaise aaye?*" ~ "So how did you find your way to our small cricket academy?" he asked, gesturing for me to follow him to the shade of a large tree where we could talk while he kept an eye on the practice.

As we settled on a bench made from a rough-hewn log, Coach Anil shared the academy's story. Fifteen years ago, he had been a promising cricketer himself, playing at the state level but never quite breaking through to the national team. When his playing days ended, he returned to his hometown determined to create opportunities for local children that he never had.

"*Shuruat mein sirf paanch bachche the. Ab 50 se zyada hain, different age groups mein*" ~ "Initially there were only five children. Now there are more than 50, in different age groups" he explained, his eyes never leaving the field as he spoke. "*Lekin sponsorship ya funding? Kuch nahi.*" ~ "But sponsorship or funding? Nothing."

The academy operated on a shoestring budget—mainly funded from Anil's own pocket, supplemented by voluntary contributions from parents when they could afford it. Many children paid nothing at all. Equipment was donated, repaired repeatedly, and shared among all players.

"*Mere paas paisa nahi hai, facilities nahi hai. Par agar yeh junoon kisi ladke ka sapna poora kar sake, toh bas yahi meri jeet hai*" ~ "I don't have money or facilities. But if this passion helps even one child fulfill their dream, that's my victory," he said, his voice reflecting the same quiet conviction I had seen in his posture.

What struck me most about Coach Anil wasn't just his dedication but his approach. As he pointed out different children, explaining their strengths and areas for improvement, I realized he knew each one not just as a player but as a person—their family circumstances, their school performance, their individual challenges.

"*Cricket sirf khel nahi hai. Life lessons hai*" ~ "Cricket isn't just a game. It's life's lessons," he said. "*Discipline, teamwork, handling pressure, bouncing back from failure—yeh sab cricket sikhata hai.*" ~ "Discipline, teamwork, handling pressure, bouncing back from failure—cricket teaches all this."

The Children's Stories

As we watched the practice session, Coach Anil introduced me to the stories behind some of his most committed players:

Rahul: Playing Through Pain

A thirteen-year-old boy was batting in the nets with remarkable concentration. What I hadn't noticed until Coach Anil pointed it out was that his right index finger was heavily bandaged.

"*Uski ungli fracture hui thi do hafta pehle. Doctor ne khelna mana kiya, par usne practice nahi chhodi*" ~ "His finger was fractured two weeks ago. The doctor forbade him to play, but he didn't stop practicing," the coach explained with a mixture of concern and pride. "*Kehta hai—sirf dard hai. Khelenge toh jayega.*" ~ "He says—it's just pain. If I keep playing, it'll go away."

Rahul came from a family of four living in a two-room house. His father worked as a taxi driver, often taking tourists to nearby McLeod Ganj. Despite financial constraints, his parents supported his cricket dreams, believing it could provide opportunities beyond their circumstances.

"*Usme talent hai, dedication hai, aur sabse important—hunger hai. Woh apne situation se bahar nikalna chahta hai*" ~ "He has talent, dedication, and most importantly—hunger. He wants to escape his situation," Coach Anil observed.

Priya: Breaking Boundaries

Among the boys, one figure stood out—a 12-year-old girl named Priya, practicing her batting with a technique that many boys her age would envy. Her stance was textbook perfect, her backswing precise, her footwork assured.

"*Log kehte hain ladkiyon ke liye cricket nahi hai. Par jab mai shot maar deti hoon, toh woh chup ho jaate hain*" ~ "People say cricket isn't for girls. But when I hit my shots, they went silent," she had told Coach Anil when she first joined the academy.

The daughter of a school teacher, Priya had grown up watching cricket with her father. When she expressed interest in playing rather than just watching, many neighborhood boys had mocked her. But Coach Anil welcomed her without hesitation.

"*Talent has no gender,*" he said in English, before switching back to Hindi. "*Aur woh talented hai. Bohot zyada.*" ~ "And she is talented. Very much so."

According to Anil, Priya was now one of his most disciplined students—always first to arrive and last to leave, practicing her technique with a dedication that put many of the boys to shame. Her dream was to emulate Smriti Mandhana, the star of India's women's cricket team.

"*Women's cricket ab recognize ho raha hai India mein. Priya ka time aayega*" ~ "Women's cricket is now being recognized in India. Priya's time will come," Anil said with conviction.

Karan: The Long Walk to Dreams

As practice continued, Coach Anil pointed out a tall, thin boy of about fifteen who was bowling with impressive speed.

"*Woh Karan hai. Roz 10-kilometer paidal aata hai yahan practice karne*" ~ "That's Karan. He walks 10 kilometers every day to practice here," he said.

Karan lived in a village in the hills with no direct transportation to Dharamshala. His family couldn't afford a bicycle, let alone a bus pass. So, every day, rain or shine, he walked five kilometers each way to attend practice.

"*Ghar pe paisa nahi hai bus ya cycle ke liye. Par mai chal sakta hoon*" ~ We don't have money for a bus or cycle at home. But I can walk," Karan had told Coach Anil when asked about his long commute.

His determination had paid off in his developing skill as a fast bowler. According to Coach Anil, several district-level coaches had already noticed Karan's natural talent and raw speed.

"*Uske andar fire hai*" ~ "There's fire inside him," Anil said simply. "*Aur saath mein control bhi. Yeh combination bahut rare hai.*" ~ "And with it, control. This combination is very rare."

Cricket Philosophy During the Break

As the practice session paused for a water break, the children gathered under the shade trees, rehydrating and catching their breath. I was invited to join them and soon found myself in the middle of an animated discussion about cricket legends.

What surprised me was the sophistication of their cricket knowledge. These children—many of whom had limited formal education and no access to the internet—discussed cricket history, technique, and strategy with the expertise of professional commentators.

"*Aap ke favorite cricketer kaun hain?*" ~ "Who is your favorite cricketer?" Aditya, a tall 16-year-old, asked me politely.

Before I could answer, the group erupted into their own passionate nominations—Virat Kohli, MS Dhoni, Rohit Sharma, and other contemporary stars.

But what truly impressed me was when the conversation shifted to cricket history and philosophy. A shorter boy, perhaps 14 years old, spoke up with unexpected insight:

"*Mujhe Tendulkar aur Gavaskar pasand hai. Unhone bhi yahi kiya—jo mila uska behtareen istemal kiya*" ~ "I like Tendulkar and Gavaskar. They did the same—made the best use of what they got," he explained thoughtfully.

He went on to analyze how both Tendulkar and Gavaskar had succeeded despite being shorter than many international batsmen—compensating with technique, timing, and mental strength rather than physical advantage.

"*Height kam thi, par skill zyada thi*" ~ "Height was less, but skill was more," he concluded with wisdom beyond his years.

Others joined in, discussing:

- **Kapil Dev's** courage and perseverance against the fearsome West Indian pace attacks of the 1980s
- **Mohinder Amarnath's** comeback after being hit repeatedly by bouncers, showing mental toughness
- **Rahul Dravid's** patience and technical perfection, earning him the nickname "The Wall"
- **Jhulan Goswami's** journey from a small Bengal village to becoming the world's leading wicket-taker in women's ODIs
- **Smriti Mandhana's** elegant batting style that disproved stereotypes about women's cricket

I sat amazed, listening to these children from remote Himalayan foothills discussing cricket with a depth that many professional analysts would envy. They didn't just admire players for their statistics or celebrity status— they understood the deeper narratives of struggle, adaptation, and perseverance behind the achievements.

Coach Anil watched with quiet pride, occasionally adding context or correcting facts, but mostly allowing the children to express their understanding. I could see how he had cultivated not just technical skills but a philosophical approach to the game—teaching his students to look beyond boundaries and centuries to the character that produced them.

More Than Just Cricket

As the water break ended and practice resumed, I remained with Coach Anil, watching the children return to their drills with renewed energy.

"*Aapko pata hai*" ~ "You know," he said after a few moments of silence, "*inme se shayad ek ya do hi professional cricketers banenge. Baaki sab doctor, engineer, teacher, ya kuch aur banenge.*" ~ "Maybe only one or two of them will become professional cricketers. The rest will become doctors, engineers, teachers, or something else."

This wasn't said with disappointment but with realistic understanding. Cricket, like most professional sports, is a pyramid with a very narrow top. Even with talent and dedication, the odds of reaching international level are extremely slim.

"*Par cricket khelne se jo seekhenge, woh zindagi bhar kaam aayega*" ~ "But what they learn from playing cricket will help them throughout life," he continued. "*Hard work, discipline, team spirit, pressure handle karna—yeh sab skills hain jo kaheen bhi useful hongi.*" ~ "Hard work, discipline, team spirit, handling pressure—these are all skills that will be useful anywhere."

What Coach Anil had created went far beyond a cricket academy. It was a life school disguised as sports training—a place where children from modest backgrounds could develop qualities that would serve them regardless of their eventual careers.

I watched as Priya, after being bowled out in practice, immediately analyzed her footwork error and requested another chance. I observed Karan helping a younger boy adjust his bowling grip. I noticed Rahul, despite his injury, volunteering to field in a difficult position.

These weren't just cricket skills being developed; they were character traits being forged—resilience, generosity, courage, and the pursuit of excellence regardless of circumstances.

"*Cricket inko discipline sikhata hai, lekin saath mein dreaming bhi sikhata hai*" ~ "Cricket teaches them discipline, but it also teaches them dreaming," Coach Anil said, summing up his philosophy. "*Aur dono zaroori hain—discipline without dreams is just control, dreams without discipline are just wishes.*"

The Seeds of Future Greatness

As the afternoon practice session ended, the children gathered for a final huddle before dispersing to their homes. Coach Anil spoke briefly to them, not about cricket techniques but about their upcoming school exams—reminding them that their studies were as important as their sports.

They broke the huddle with an enthusiastic team cheer, then began the ritual of cleaning up the field and storing equipment. Even in this mundane activity, I noticed their sense of ownership and responsibility—these children treated the humble ground and modest equipment with the same respect professionals might show to a world-class stadium.

As they began to depart— some in groups, others alone, each heading back to their own reality beyond this field of dreams— I felt a certainty grow within me:

One day, one of these children would make it.

One day, a name I had heard on this simple field would appear in newspaper headlines. One day, a technique I had watched being practiced here would be displayed on international broadcasts. One day, a journey that began with barefoot training in the Himalayan foothills would culminate at Lord's or Eden Gardens or the Melbourne Cricket Ground.

But even if that particular dream remained elusive, something equally valuable was already being achieved here every day. In this academy with no sponsorships, no fancy facilities, and no guaranteed outcomes, children were discovering their own potential—learning that limitations need not define them, that passion can overcome circumstance, and that dreams pursued with discipline are always worth the journey.

As I thanked Coach Anil and prepared to leave, he smiled and gestured toward his departing students.

"*Cricket ke through inko ek message milta hai—ki background, paisa, ya privilege se zyada important hai dedication aur belief*" ~ "Through cricket, they get a message—that more important than background, money, or privilege are dedication and belief," he said. "*Aur yeh lesson cricket se bhi bara hai.*" ~ "And this lesson is bigger than cricket."

Walking back toward town as the sun began to set behind the mountains, I carried with me the image of those children playing with pure joy and fierce determination on their simple ground—a reminder that greatness often takes root in the most unlikely places, nurtured not by abundance but by the power of human spirit against all odds.

Chapter 13:
The Weather Within

The Climate of Life

Weather is more than just a conversation starter.

It shapes our days, influences our moods, and becomes a mirror to our inner states. Rain can be tears or cleansing. Wind can be chaos or freedom. Sunshine can be hope or harsh exposure.

During my journey across India after selling my Mercedes, I experienced the country not just through its people and places, but through its remarkably diverse weather patterns. Each city's climate created a distinct rhythm of life, forcing different adaptations, teaching different lessons, and revealing different aspects of human resilience.

In Mumbai's drowning monsoons, Delhi's bone-chilling winters, Chennai's relentless heat, and Bangalore's gentle breezes, I discovered that weather isn't just something we endure—it's something we internalize. The way people respond to external conditions often reflects their approach to life's broader challenges.

This chapter is about those connections—about the weather outside and the weather within, about how climate shapes culture, and about the wisdom found in adapting to forces beyond our control.

Mumbai's Monsoon: The Drowning and the Dancing

My first experience of Mumbai's infamous monsoon came without warning. One moment, I was walking down a busy street under gray but dry skies; the next, heaven crashed down.

This wasn't gentle rain. This was a vertical ocean, falling with such intensity that the sound alone was disorienting. Within seconds, I was drenched to the skin, my clothes clinging to my body, water streaming down my face, and my vision blurred. Around me, the street transformed—shallow pools became puddles, puddles became ponds, and gutters became rushing rivers carrying debris and hopes away with equal indifference.

Most striking was how quickly Mumbai segregated into two distinct groups of people: those who ran for cover, huddling in doorways and under awnings, waiting for nature to relent; and those who simply continued—walking, working, and living as if the deluge were merely an inconvenience rather than an impediment.

At Churchgate Station, I took shelter under the overhanging roof, watching as commuters streamed in and out despite the downpour. Here I met Yusuf, a newspaper vendor who had been selling papers at the same spot for over twenty years. While other vendors had closed their shops, Yusuf continued his business, his newspapers protected by an ingenious system of plastic sheets and an angled wooden platform that kept the water at bay.

"*Baarish se darr ke ghar baithne wale Mumbai mein jee nahi sakte*" ~ "Those who fear the rain and sit at home cannot survive in Mumbai," he told me with a knowing smile, adjusting his plastic covering as he spoke. "*Yahan paani girta hai, par zindagi rukti nahi hai.*" ~ "Here, water falls, but life doesn't stop."

Yusuf explained that he had developed his waterproofing techniques through years of trial and error. Early in his career, he had lost the entire stack of newspapers to unexpected downpours, sometimes representing a week's income. Rather than accept this as inevitable, he had studied how water flowed, where it pooled, and how to channel it away from his precious inventory.

"*Adaptation is survival*," he said in surprisingly good English, before switching back to Hindi. "*Jo adjust nahi kar sakta, woh Mumbai mein tik nahi sakta.*" ~ "Those who cannot adjust, cannot last in Mumbai."

What fascinated me about Yusuf and others like him wasn't just their practical adaptations but their philosophical ones. The monsoon wasn't an enemy to be resisted or fled from—it was simply a reality to be accommodated, a condition of existence that required specific responses.

As I watched the crowd outside the station, I noticed a young couple deliberately jumping into a large puddle, laughing as water splashed around them. Nearby, a group of children had turned a flooded side street into an impromptu swimming pool, their joy palpable in the midst of what many would consider miserable conditions.

For these Mumbaikars, the monsoon was not merely endured—it was embraced, celebrated, even enjoyed. The same rain that flooded homes and disrupted lives also provided relief from heat, replenished water supplies, and created moments of unexpected beauty as raindrops caught light.

Yet this romantic view existed alongside harsh realities. For the wealthy, monsoon meant inconvenience—perhaps a canceled dinner plan, a longer commute, or water seeping into luxury cars. For the poor, especially those living in slums or on the streets, it meant existential threat—homes washed away, possessions ruined, diseases spreading through contaminated water, and livelihoods temporarily destroyed.

The same rain fell on everyone, but its impact varied dramatically based on privilege and position.

Despite these disparities, Mumbai displayed a collective resilience that transcended class divisions. The famous dabbawalas still delivered thousands of lunch boxes with remarkable precision, wading through flooded streets to ensure office workers received their home-cooked meals. Street vendors still hawked umbrellas, raincoats, and hot chai to drenched passersby. Construction workers still balanced on scaffolding, their already dangerous jobs made more precarious by slippery surfaces and reduced visibility.

The city refused to pause, refused to yield to nature's onslaught.

While my instinct as an outsider was to seek shelter and wait for better conditions, Mumbai taught me that sometimes the only way forward is through. The monsoon became a metaphor for life's inevitable deluges—those periods of overwhelming challenge that seem to drown us in problems.

We can hide and hope they pass, or we can learn to dance in the rain, find joy in the puddles, and keep moving forward even when soaked to the bone.

Delhi's Winter: The Numbing and the Warming

If Mumbai's monsoon was a test of adaptability, Delhi's winter was a lesson in contrast—both external and internal.

I arrived in the capital during December, when the city was in the grip of its annual deep freeze. The moment I stepped off the train at New Delhi Railway Station, the bone-chilling cold hit me with physical force. The air had a brittle quality, each breath bringing a sharp pain to my lungs unused to such temperatures.

Early mornings were particularly striking. A thick fog enveloped the city, transforming familiar landmarks into ghostly apparitions. The famous India Gate would appear and disappear as if playing hide-and-seek with observers. Historic tombs and monuments emerged from the mist like structures from another time, their outlines softened and made mysterious by the swirling gray.

This eerie backdrop created an atmosphere unlike any other Indian city—a quieter, more contemplative Delhi where sounds were muffled and distances deceiving.

Near Connaught Place one evening, I met Babulal, an elderly peanut seller whose small cart featured a brazier of glowing coals that served the dual purpose of roasting nuts and providing warmth. His hands were rough and cracked from exposure, his thin frame wrapped in multiple layers of clothing, his breath visible as small clouds in the cold air.

As I purchased a packet of hot peanuts, I asked how he managed to work in such harsh conditions day after day.

"*Garibi ka mausam humesha sardi jaisa hota hai—insaan ko andar se thanda kar deta hai*" ~ "Poverty always feels like winter—it numbs you from the inside," he replied, his voice scratchy but his eyes still bright. "*Bas, hum adjust kar lete hain. Bahar ki thand se andar ki thand zyada takleef deti hai.*" ~ "We just adjust. The cold inside hurts more than the cold outside."

His philosophical perspective struck me deeply. For Babulal, the physical winter was merely an external manifestation of the constant internal winter of poverty. Yet despite this double burden, he maintained both his livelihood and his dignity, his small fire a defiance against both natural and economic chills.

Delhi's winter created physical layers—people wrapped themselves in woolen shawls, mufflers, caps, and gloves, moving through the city as bundled silhouettes against the gray backdrop. But it also revealed emotional and social layers that remained hidden in other seasons.

The privileged retreated to homes with heaters, restaurants with climate control, and cars with warm seats. The poor created ingenious adaptations—newspaper insulation inside thin clothing, communal bonfires at street corners, shared bodily warmth in crowded shelters.

Yet amid this stratification emerged unexpected moments of connection. At roadside tea stalls, people from different backgrounds huddled together around small stoves, their social distinctions temporarily thawed by shared need for warmth. The rich might arrive in luxury cars and the poor on foot, but for a few minutes, they stood shoulder to shoulder, cradling hot cups in cold hands, their breath mingling in the frigid air.

Delhi's winter also brought unique rituals and sensory experiences. The aroma of kebabs grilling over open flames. The crackling sound of Lohri bonfires celebrating the harvest and winter solstice. The striking vision of Republic Day celebrations proceeding through fog, military precision somehow maintained despite limited visibility.

Most impressive was Delhi's refusal to hibernate. Even in the coldest predawn hours, the city maintained its pulse. Rickshaw pullers pedaled through empty streets; their thin blankets wrapped around their shoulders as they sought early morning passengers. Chai vendors fired up their stoves while stars still shone in the dark sky. Street musicians played flutes and harmoniums with half-frozen fingers near temple entrances.

Life continued not despite winter but alongside it—adapting, accommodating, finding warmth where possible and enduring where necessary.

I realized that what was true of Delhi's winter was equally true of life's difficult seasons. When faced with periods of emotional coldness, loss, or hardship, we have similar choices—to retreat and protect ourselves, to seek warmth in community, or to find that inner fire that keeps us moving forward even when everything around us seems frozen.

The most resilient, like Babulal, somehow maintain that inner flame regardless of external conditions.

Chennai's Heat: The Forging and the Focusing

Chennai greeted me with a heat so different from Delhi's cold that it seemed to belong to another planet, not just another city. This wasn't just high temperature; it was physical pressure—a weight of warmth that pressed against skin, forced its way into lungs, and seemed to slow time itself.

Walking Chennai's streets at midday felt like moving through invisible molasses. Each step required extra effort, each breath delivered air that offered little relief. Sweat didn't just appear; it poured, soaking clothes within minutes and creating a constant state of dampness that became a second skin.

Under this relentless thermal assault, the city developed its own distinct rhythm—a more measured pace than Mumbai's frenzy or Delhi's structured hustle. People moved with deliberate steps, conserving energy, finding shadow paths along buildings, creating makeshift cooling systems with wet cloths and hand fans.

Near the Kapaleeshwarar Temple in Mylapore, I encountered Lakshmi, a flower seller whose small stall offered garlands of jasmine, rose, and marigold for temple offerings. Despite the crushing heat, her fingers moved with remarkable dexterity, threading flowers into intricate patterns without pause or error.

"*Aap is garmi mein kaise kaam kar leti hain?*" “How do you work in this heat?” I asked, wiping sweat from my forehead for the dozenth time that hour.

She looked up briefly from her work, her expression suggesting my question was slightly absurd.

"*Garmi sirf shareer ko takleef deti hai, mann ko nahi*" ~ “The heat only troubles the body, not the mind,” she replied simply. "*Mann ko focus rakhna seekhna padta hai, chahe bahar kaisa bhi mausam ho.*" ~ “One must learn to keep the mind focused, regardless of the weather outside.”

Her answer wasn't merely philosophical; it was practical wisdom born of necessity. In Chennai's climate, those who allowed the heat to penetrate their concentration couldn't survive economically. Lakshmi had trained herself to create a mental space untouched by physical discomfort— a skill as valuable as her flower-threading technique.

This separation of physical sensation from mental focus was something I observed repeatedly throughout Chennai. At construction sites, workers labored under the direct sun, their bodies glistening with sweat but their attention undivided from their tasks. In markets, vendors maintained good humor and sharp business acumen despite conditions that would drive many to distraction or irritability.

Chennai's heat had forged a particular kind of resilience in its people—a capacity for patience, discipline, and endurance that became part of the cultural character. Unlike

Mumbai's dramatic adaptation to monsoons or Delhi's layered response to winter, Chennai's approach to heat was more internal than external, more about mental discipline than physical adjustment.

Yet creativity emerged even here. People developed ingenious cooling mechanisms—from traditional clay pots that kept water naturally cool to precisely placed dwellings that caught whatever breeze might pass. Social customs evolved around the climate—predawn activities, afternoon siestas, and a vibrant night life when temperatures finally relented.

Most striking was how the heat influenced interpersonal dynamics. Conversations tended to be more measured and thoughtful, with less of the rapid-fire exchange found in other cities. People listened more carefully, perhaps because the effort to speak made words more valuable. Conflicts seemed to simmer rather than boil over, as if the external heat absorbed some of the internal variety.

As days passed, I found myself adapting not just physically but mentally to Chennai's climate. I began to appreciate the way heat slowed my thoughts, forced me to be more deliberate in my actions, and created a kind of meditative state where only the essential mattered.

In a world of constant distraction and acceleration, Chennai's heat-enforced patience offered its own wisdom—teaching me that sometimes the most powerful response to overwhelming conditions is not resistance but a calm, centered focus that acknowledges difficulty without being defined by it.

Bangalore's Breeze: The Pausing and the Creating

After the extremes of Mumbai's floods, Delhi's freeze, and Chennai's furnace, arriving in Bangalore felt like an exhalation. The city's famous climate—moderate temperatures, gentle breezes, and misty mornings—created a physical reprieve that seemed to extend to the city's entire character.

My first morning there, I woke early and walked through Cubbon Park as dawn broke. A light mist hovered just above the ground, giving the trees an otherworldly quality. The air had a crispness that invited deep breathing, a freshness that seemed to clear not just the lungs but thoughts.

This wasn't weather that demanded adaptation or resistance; it was weather that invited appreciation and presence. For the first time in my journey, I wasn't fighting external conditions but being gently supported by them.

The effect this climate had on Bangalore's rhythm was immediately apparent. People moved with less urgency but more purpose. Outdoor spaces have become natural extensions of indoor ones, with parks, street corners, and rooftop cafés filled with conversations that could linger without discomfort.

In Indiranagar, I spent an afternoon at a café where young entrepreneurs worked on laptops, discussed business plans, and sketched ideas on napkins. The open-air setting, with ceiling fans barely needed in the pleasant air, created an atmosphere conducive to both concentration and creativity.

I struck up a conversation with Kiran, who had recently left a corporate job to start his own design firm. When I asked what had influenced his decision, his answer surprised me.

"*I realized that life isn't about running on someone else's schedule. Sometimes, you must pause, breathe, and find your own rhythm,*" he explained, gesturing toward the street outside where people walked at a noticeably more relaxed pace than in other Indian metros.

Bangalore's climate seemed to have infused its innovation culture with a particular quality—one that valued reflection alongside action, contemplation alongside execution. The city was ambitious but not frantic, forward-looking but present-focused.

Unlike other tech hubs that glorified constant hustle and sleep deprivation, Bangalore's startup scene had a more sustainable energy. People worked hard but also stepped away, enabled by a climate that made outdoor breaks genuinely refreshing rather than another endurance test.

As I walked the city's streets, I noticed how the pleasant weather democratized public space in ways impossible elsewhere. In a small neighborhood park, elderly men played chess in the shade of banyan trees. On a grassy median, young college students sat studying together. Outside an office building, a team meeting happened informally on benches rather than in a conference room.

The climate fostered a kind of collective pause—not idleness, but intentional spaciousness that allowed thoughts to develop and connections to form without the pressure of extreme conditions forcing quick decisions or retreats to private spaces.

Most revelatory was the understanding that not every moment must be a struggle. After weeks of battling elements in other cities, Bangalore's gentleness reminded me that progress doesn't always require fighting against conditions. Sometimes, growth happens most effectively when we are supported rather than challenged by our environment.

In professional and personal development, we often value the struggle, believing that difficult conditions necessarily produce stronger results. Bangalore's climate and culture suggested an alternative wisdom—that creativity, innovation, and human connection might sometimes flourish best not in the forge of hardship but in the garden of supportive conditions.

This didn't mean Bangalore lacked challenges or that its pleasant climate translated to an easy life for all its residents. The city had its own social problems, inequalities, and difficulties. But the backdrop against which these challenges played out created different possibilities for addressing them—more space for reflection, greater opportunity for public discourse, less energy consumed by mere survival.

The Weather as Teacher

As my journey across India neared its conclusion, I reflected on how profoundly weather had shaped not just my experiences but my understanding of human resilience and adaptation.

Each climate had offered its own wisdom:

Mumbai's monsoon taught me that some storms must be moved through rather than waited out, and that there is grace in adaptation rather than resistance.

Delhi's winter showed me how external coldness can either numb us or awaken our appreciation for warmth in all its forms—physical, social, and spiritual.

Chennai's heat demonstrated the power of mental discipline, of separating internal focus from external conditions, of maintaining clarity even when surrounded by discomfort.

Bangalore's breeze reminded me that not every season needs to be a battle, that there is wisdom in pause, and that supportive conditions can nurture different kinds of growth than challenging ones.

Together, these weather patterns became metaphors for life's varying seasons—times of overwhelming challenge, periods of isolation and coldness, stretches of relentless pressure, and moments of supportive ease.

What stays with me is not just the extremity of India's weather but the remarkable human responses to it—the creativity, adaptation, resilience, and wisdom that emerge when people must coexist with forces far beyond their control.

Perhaps that is the deepest lesson of all: we cannot choose the external conditions of our lives any more than we can command the rain to stop or the sun to cool, but we can choose how we respond to those conditions—whether we curse the rain or dance in it, whether we let the cold freeze our hearts or find ways to share our warmth, whether we surrender to heat or find focus within it, whether we appreciate gentle days as opportunities for reflection and connection.

The weather without shapes the weather within, but never completely determines it.

As I prepare to return to my life after these months of wandering, I carry with me not just memories of places and people, but a deeper understanding of how to navigate life's inevitable storms, chills, heat waves, and gentle breezes—with resilience, adaptation, focus, and gratitude for each season's distinct gifts.

Chapter 14: Lessons from the Journey

From Experiment to Awakening

What began as an experiment had become a transformation.

When I first sold my Mercedes at a loss and stepped into the world of public transportation, I had approached it almost like a social project—a temporary adventure to broaden my perspective before returning to my comfortable corporate cocoon. I thought I would observe life from a different angle, collect some interesting stories, and perhaps gain some insight into how "the other half" lived.

I had no idea that the journey would fundamentally change me.

Now, as I prepared to complete my six-month exploration, I found myself reflecting on the stark contrast between the isolated luxury I had left behind and the immersive experience I had embraced. My air-conditioned car with tinted windows had kept me comfortable but separate—floating through India rather than being part of it. The buses, trains, shared autos, and countless footsteps of my journey had placed me firmly within the flow of life, with all its discomforts, joys, and profound connections.

The lessons I had learned weren't academic observations but lived experiences that had seeped into my bones, reshaping not just what I knew but who I was. They weren't lessons about "others" but about humanity itself—including my own.

This chapter is about those lessons—the wisdom gathered not from books or seminars but from rain-soaked streets, crowded train compartments, sweltering afternoons, and countless conversations with people I would have never met from behind the wheel of my Mercedes.

First Lesson: Resilience - Making Opportunity from Difficulty

Mumbai taught me the first and perhaps most fundamental lesson: true resilience isn't about enduring hardship but transforming it into opportunity.

During a particularly heavy monsoon downpour that had turned streets into shallow rivers, I took shelter under the awning of a shop near Dadar Station. There I noticed a young girl, perhaps fourteen or fifteen, who had set up a small makeshift stall selling plastic covers for mobile phones and wallets.

Meenal, as she introduced herself, had positioned her business precisely where people would be most concerned about protecting their valuables from water damage. Rather than seeing the rain as an obstacle to commerce, she had recognized it as the perfect selling condition for her product.

"*Baarish rukegi toh dukaan band hojayegi, bhaiya*" ~ "If the rain stops, my shop will close, brother," she laughed when I commented on her clever positioning. "*Har problem, opportunity hai—bas nazar sahi jagah pe rakhni padti hai.*" ~ "Every problem is an opportunity—you just need to look in the right place."

She had turned selling waterproof covers into a game, challenging passersby to see if their devices could survive the monsoon without her protection. Her playful banter and entrepreneurial spirit attracted customers who might otherwise have hurried past, heads down against the rain.

Meenal's approach exemplified what I saw repeatedly throughout Mumbai—people who refused to surrender to circumstances and instead found creative ways to navigate and even leverage them.

The rickshaw driver whose vehicle stalled in flood water quickly converted it to a push-cart service for stranded commuters. The chai vendor who attached a simple tarp system to his stall that collected rainwater and redirected it away from his customers. Even the beggar near the train station who offered to hold umbrellas for people while they searched for tickets or arranged their bags—earning tips for solving a problem created by the very conditions that made his usual begging more difficult.

None of these individuals merely endured the monsoon; they engaged with it, adapted to it, and sometimes even profited from it. Their resilience wasn't passive acceptance but active response—a refusal to be defined as victims of circumstance.

This lesson followed me throughout my journey. Whenever I faced discomfort or inconvenience, I found myself thinking of Meenal's laugh and her clear-eyed recognition that within every problem lies a potential opportunity. Resilience, I learned, is not about gritting your teeth and bearing hardship— it's about maintaining the flexibility and creativity to transform difficult conditions into new possibilities.

Second Lesson: Kindness - Finding Warmth in Cold Places

Delhi's bitter winter revealed a second powerful lesson: true kindness isn't an occasional grand gesture but a daily choice that requires no recognition.

On one particularly frigid January evening near India Gate, I noticed an elderly man methodically distributing blankets to homeless people who had gathered at a nearby park. He wasn't part of any organization— no charity logos, no assistants, no photography documenting his good deeds. Just a solitary figure with a small handcart stacked with woolen blankets, moving quietly from person to person.

Curious, I approached and offered to help. He accepted with a nod but seemed reluctant to engage in conversation about his work. When I asked his name, wanting to acknowledge his generosity, he gently deflected.

"*Mujhe koi naam ya dhanyawad nahi chahiye, beta*" ~ "I don't want recognition or gratitude, son," he explained softly. "*Jab insaan thand mein hota hai, toh sirf ek hi dua maangta hai—ki koi use garam rakh le.*" ~ "When a person is in the cold, they only pray for warmth."

He had been providing blankets for three winters, purchasing them with his own modest pension. His actions weren't motivated by religious obligation or social recognition but by the simple recognition of human need and his own capacity to address it.

Throughout Delhi, I witnessed similar small acts of kindness that created warmth in the coldest season:

A rickshaw puller gave free rides to elderly women struggling to walk on icy streets.

A woman at a bus stop unwrapped her own shawl to share with a young mother whose baby was underdressed for the unexpected temperature drop.

A tea seller kept a pot of chai brewing through the night, allowing a shivering street boy to warm his hands against the pot even when he couldn't afford a cup.

These weren't wealthy philanthropists or social activists with resources to spare. They were ordinary people, often struggling themselves, who chose to share what little they had without expectation of return or recognition.

What struck me most was how these small kindnesses created a chain reaction. People who received unexpected warmth—whether physical or emotional—seemed more likely to extend it to others. A blanket given freely one night might inspire its recipient to share food the next day. A moment of compassion spawned other moments, creating ripples of warmth in the coldest conditions.

The elderly blanket distributor taught me that kindness in its purest form requires no audience, no gratitude, no recognition— only the simple acknowledgment that we are all vulnerable to the cold, and we all have some capacity, however small, to provide warmth to others.

Third Lesson: Endurance - Being Forged Rather Than Burned

Chennai's relentless heat delivered a third crucial lesson: true endurance isn't just about surviving difficulty but allowing it to strengthen you.

I remembered Lakshmi, the flower seller near Kapaleeshwarar Temple, whose fingers worked with remarkable precision despite temperatures that left me barely able to think clearly. Day after day, she sat in the same spot, threading jasmine blossoms into garlands with unfaltering focus.

"*Garmi sirf shareer ko takleef deti hai, mann ko nahi*" ~ "The heat only troubles the body, not the mind," she had told me when I marveled at her concentration in such conditions.

Lakshmi hadn't merely developed tolerance for the heat; she had trained herself to transcend it mentally—to acknowledge physical discomfort without allowing it to disrupt her internal focus. This wasn't just passive endurance but active mental discipline.

Throughout Chennai, I observed this same quality in countless individuals:

The vegetable vendors maintained their good humor and sharp business acumen during the most scorching middays.

The auto drivers navigated crowded streets hour after hour, their concentration unwavering despite the sweat streaming down their faces.

The temple priests performed elaborate rituals in heavy traditional garments, their movements precise and dignified regardless of the temperature.

What these individuals shared wasn't just physical stamina but a particular mental approach—a capacity to distinguish between unavoidable external conditions and their internal response to those conditions. They didn't deny the heat's reality, but they refused to grant it power over their focus, mood, or effectiveness.

Chennai taught me that true endurance goes beyond mere survival or "putting up with" difficult circumstances. It involves a conscious choice to be forged rather than burned by challenging conditions—to use them as opportunities for developing mental discipline and inner strength.

This lesson proved valuable far beyond dealing with physical heat. When facing challenging situations of any kind—emotional stress, work pressure, relationship difficulties—I began to practice the mental separation Lakshmi had demonstrated. I could acknowledge discomfort without being defined by it, recognize difficulty without being diminished by it.

Chennai's heat, in teaching me how to maintain internal focus despite external pressure, had given me a tool for navigating life's inevitable difficult seasons with greater equanimity and effectiveness.

Fourth Lesson: Breathing - Finding Your Own Rhythm

Bangalore's gentle climate and more measured pace offered a fourth essential lesson: progress doesn't always require struggle, and sometimes the most productive thing we can do is pause.

I recalled Kiran, the young entrepreneur I had met at a café in Indiranagar, who had left his high-pressure corporate job to start his own design firm. His decision wasn't driven by the desire for greater wealth or status but by the recognition that he needed space to think, create, and work at a rhythm that suited his natural temperament.

"*I realized that life isn't about running on someone else's schedule,*" he had explained. "*Sometimes, you have to pause, breathe, and find your own rhythm.*"

Throughout Bangalore, I encountered others who had made similar choices:

The artists in Cubbon Park would spend hours sketching, seemingly unconcerned with productivity metrics or output quotas.

The tech professionals had deliberately chosen smaller companies or freelance work that allowed them greater control over their pace and focus.

The retirees gathered for morning walks and philosophical discussions, finding meaning not in continued achievement but in reflection and connection.

Bangalore's pleasant climate seemed to create space for a particular kind of wisdom—one that valued purposeful pauses, thoughtful consideration, and individual rhythms over constant action or standardized pace.

After months of witnessing incredible human resilience against adversity in other cities, Bangalore reminded me that not all growth comes through struggle. Sometimes the most significant development happens when we step away from the fight-or-flight urgency of daily challenges and create space for reflection, integration, and mindful choice.

This lesson challenged my deeply ingrained belief that progress always required effort, struggle, and constant forward motion. I began to recognize the value of breathing spaces—not as retreats from life but as essential components of a well-lived one.

Bangalore taught me that finding and honoring your own natural rhythm isn't indulgence or weakness; it's a form of wisdom that can lead to more sustainable growth, greater creativity, and more authentic contributions than constantly pushing against your nature or capabilities.

Fifth Lesson: Mirroring - The Journey Within

As my six-month exploration neared its conclusion, I recognized perhaps the most profound lesson of all: every journey outward is also a journey inward, with each place we visit revealing different aspects of ourselves.

The final leg of my trip involved a long train ride back toward my starting point. As I watched fields and towns pass by the window, I reflected on how each city had not only taught me about its people but had also revealed different dimensions of my own character and values.

Mumbai had exposed my hunger for security and control, challenging me to develop greater comfort with uncertainty and chaos.

Delhi had confronted me with my tendencies toward self-protection and emotional distance, inviting more authentic connection and shared vulnerability.

Chennai had highlighted my reactivity to discomfort, teaching me greater equanimity and mental discipline.

Bangalore had revealed my addiction to busyness and achievement, reminding me of the value of presence and reflection.

Each place had acted as a mirror, showing me not just external realities but internal patterns I might never have recognized in the comfortable isolation of my previous life. The journey had been circular in an unexpected way—starting with the desire to understand others better and ending with a deeper understanding of myself.

The train's steady rhythm matched my contemplative mood as I considered how profoundly my perspective had shifted. People I would once have pitied now seemed worthy of admiration. Situations I would have avoided now appeared rich with opportunity. Comforts I had considered essential now felt optional, even sometimes obstructive to genuine experience.

I realized that selling my Mercedes had never really been about transportation at all. It had been about transformation—about removing the barriers that kept me separated from the world and from parts of myself. The loss I had accepted on the car's sale price was trivial compared to the wealth of insight, connection, and growth I had gained in return.

As the train continued its journey through the gathering dusk, I understood that while my six-month experiment was ending, the real journey—the internal one—would continue. The lessons of resilience, kindness, endurance, rhythm, and self-knowledge weren't limited to specific locations or experiences; they were tools for navigating all of life with greater wisdom and authenticity.

The transformation that had begun with a simple decision to sell a luxury car had become something far more significant—a recalibration of values, a reconnection with humanity, and a rediscovery of aspects of myself long forgotten in the comfortable isolation of privilege.

I had set out seeking stories and had found not just narratives but wisdom—not just observations but evolution. What started as a journey through India's diverse landscapes had become a journey through the equally diverse landscapes of human experience and personal growth.

The true destination, I now understood, had never been geographic. It had been the person I would become along the way—someone with eyes more open, a heart more accessible, and a perspective forever changed by choosing to step out of the aquarium and into the vast, unpredictable, magnificent sea of real life.

Chapter 15: Riches Beyond Measure

The True Meaning of Wealth

No one would have called me poor before I sold my Mercedes.

My bank accounts were healthy, my investments sound, my place in society secure. By every conventional measure, I was wealthy— the product of decades climbing corporate ladders, making smart decisions, and accumulating the trappings of success.

Yet standing here now, at the conclusion of my six-month journey through India's crowds and chaos, heat and humanity, I understand something profound: I was impoverished in ways I never recognized.

The man who sat in that Mercedes—isolated behind tinted windows, cushioned by leather seats, separated from the world by German engineering and air conditioning—was wealthy in currency but poor in connection. Rich in comfort but lacking in experience. Prosperous in possessions but deprived of perspective.

The man who stands today—having walked these streets, traveled in these buses, and eaten at these roadside stalls—has discovered riches beyond measure. Not the kind that can be deposited in banks or displayed in driveways, but the kind that transforms how we see ourselves and our place in the world.

This final chapter is about the transformation—about the shift from measuring wealth by what we must measuring it by what we've experienced, who we've connected with, and how deeply we've lived.

Richer in Understanding

My first new form of wealth came in understanding—not the intellectual understanding that comes from books or lectures, but the bone-deep knowing that emerges only from direct experience.

I now understand the unspoken communal bonds that form in Mumbai's crowded train compartments, where strangers pressed against one another develop instant systems of support— a hand steadying someone when the train jerks, a quick warning about an approaching station, the subtle shifting that creates space for an elderly passenger.

I understand the dignity of labor that I witnessed in the rickshaw puller who, despite hours of physical exertion, maintained immaculate cleanliness in his vehicle and treated each passenger with courteous respect.

I understand the endurance of spirit displayed by the vegetable seller who sat for twelve hours in Chennai's merciless heat, arranging her produce with artistic care, knowing exactly which tomatoes would ripen by tomorrow and which must be sold today.

I understand the beauty in everyday struggles—not in a romantic, patronizing way that glorifies poverty, but in recognizing how challenges reveal human capacity for adaptation, creativity, and perseverance.

Before, I understood these realities intellectually. I could discuss economic disparities, urban challenges, or cultural resilience with well-informed opinions. But there is a vast difference between knowing something in your mind and knowing it in your body—between reading about a crowded train and standing in one for two hours, between discussing food insecurity and watching a mother divide a small portion of rice to feed multiple children.

This understanding doesn't come through observation from a distance. It comes through proximity, through the collapse of space between "them" and "me," through the recognition that humanity is not divided into categories of experience but united by them.

When I now walk past a construction worker balanced on scaffolding, I don't just see an anonymous laborer— I feel in my own muscles the strain of such work, having conversed with these workers and heard their stories. When I see a woman selling flowers outside a temple, I don't just register her as part of the scenery—I recognize the mental discipline required to maintain focus through discomfort, having witnessed it firsthand.

This understanding isn't just knowledge; it's a form of wealth that changes how I move through the world—making me more conscious of my place in it and more connected to those I share it with.

Richer in Empathy

The second form of wealth I've gained is deeper empathy—not just the ability to intellectually appreciate others' circumstances but to emotionally connect with their experiences.

I remember the woman selling idlis at dawn near a Chennai railway station. Her day began at 3 AM, preparing batter and setting up her simple stall before the first commuters arrived. I would have once seen her as an object of pity or a symbol of inequality. Now I recognize the fierce determination in her eyes, the pride in her perfectly steamed idlis, and the joy when regular customers praise her sambar's flavor.

I sat with her one morning, helping arrange banana leaves while she explained how she had put both her children through school with the earnings from this humble stall. She spoke not with resentment about her circumstances but with pride in what she had accomplished within them.

"*Mere bachche bade log banenge, aur main idli bechkar hi khush hoon*," (My children will become important people, and I am happy selling idlis) she told me, her simple statement reflecting a profound contentment in her contribution to a larger purpose.

My interaction with her and countless others has redefined success for me. I once measured it through corporate metrics— promotions earned, deals closed, assets accumulated. Now I see it in human terms—obstacles overcome, kindness maintained despite hardship, meaning created within whatever circumstances life provides.

I think of the father who sold tea eighteen hours a day to fund his daughter's engineering education, knowing she would likely move far away once educated. His success wasn't measured in his own accomplishments but in his capacity to create possibilities for someone he loved.

I remember the auto driver who maintained his smile and good humor through 14-hour shifts in Bangalore traffic, treating each passenger as if they were his first of the day rather than his fiftieth. His success wasn't financial prosperity but the daily triumph of spirit over exhaustion.

These encounters have transformed abstract concepts like "struggle" or "poverty" into human faces and stories. When I hear statistics about economic challenges, I don't just process numbers—I feel the reality of lives behind them.

This empathy doesn't drain me as I once feared it might; instead, it enriches my experience of being human, connecting me more deeply to the world around me.

This wealth of empathy has practical implications too. In business decisions, I now consider the human impact more carefully. In policy discussions, I think about how measures affect real people I've met rather than theoretical categories. In personal choices, I'm more conscious of how my actions ripple outward to affect others in ways I might once have overlooked.

Empathy, I've discovered, isn't just a virtue to cultivate—it's a form of wealth that makes life richer, making decisions wiser, and connections more meaningful.

Richer in Gratitude

Perhaps the most unexpected wealth I've gained is a profound gratitude—not just for what I have, but for what I can now see that was previously invisible to me.

I've discovered that a simple vada pav eaten in the Mumbai rain can provide more genuine satisfaction than an elaborate meal at a five-star hotel. The difference isn't in the food itself but in the entire experience—the vendor's friendly banter, the shared umbrella with a stranger, the perfect balance of spices and textures, the authenticity of the moment.

I've learned that the kindness of a stranger offering a bus seat carries more meaningful human connection than a thousand professional courtesies exchanged in corporate settings. One is a true gift given without expectation of return; the other often a transaction masked as consideration.

These realizations have transformed ordinary moments into opportunities for appreciation. A clean drink of water. A dry place during rainfall. The luxury of shade on a hot day. The wealth of having enough—not excess, just enough—to meet the day's needs.

This gratitude isn't about comparing myself favorably to those with less—a perspective that only reinforces separation. Rather, it comes from recognizing the abundance that exists in experiences I once overlooked or undervalued.

Before my journey, I was plagued by a subtle but persistent dissatisfaction—always focused on the next achievement, the next purchase, the next status symbol. Now I find myself pausing to appreciate simple pleasures: the perfect cup of roadside chai, a conversation with a stranger that shifts my perspective, the feeling of connection when sharing a laugh across language barriers.

This wealth of gratitude has freed me from the exhausting cycle of acquisition and comparison that drives so much of modern life. I still appreciate quality and beauty, but I no longer mistake them for sources of meaning or measures of worth—either my own or others'.

Instead, I've developed an eye for the extraordinary within the ordinary—the artistry in a flower seller's arrangements, the innovation in a street vendor's improvised stall, the dignity in how a rickshaw puller maintains his vehicle despite limited resources.

This gratitude isn't blind to injustice or inequality. It doesn't accept preventable suffering as inevitable or romanticize hardship. But it does recognize beauty, resilience, and meaning in places I once would have overlooked, enriching my experience of the world and my appreciation for my place within it.

The Completion of One Journey, The Beginning of Another

As I prepare to reenter my former world—to return to work, to resume old relationships, to navigate familiar environments—I recognize that while one journey is ending, another is just beginning.

The physical exploration of India's cities is complete, but the internal journey of integration and application continues. How will these experiences reshape my choices, my priorities, my interactions? How will the wealth I've gained manifest in the life I now return to?

People often ask: **"Would you buy another Mercedes now?"**

The question reflects a fundamental misunderstanding of what this journey has been about. Selling the Mercedes was never about the car itself—it was about removing the barriers that kept me separate from the world. It was a metaphor for breaking free from isolation, for choosing connection over comfort, experience over insulation.

The answer isn't about what I would or wouldn't purchase. It's about how I would approach any such decision—with greater awareness of its real impact on my life and connections, not just its symbolic value or status implications.

What matters isn't whether I ever own another luxury vehicle but whether I maintain the perspective shift that occurred when I stepped out of the last one. Will I continue to value experiences over possessions, connections over comfort, understanding over insulation? Will I remember that true wealth cannot be parked in a garage but must be lived every day through conscious choices and genuine engagement?

These are the questions that matter as one journey concludes and another begins.

True Wealth: Living Fully

When I sold my Mercedes at a loss six months ago, concerned friends and family focused on the financial implications—the depreciation I accepted, the convenience I sacrificed, the status symbol I relinquished.

What they couldn't see then— what perhaps I couldn't fully articulate myself—was the remarkable return on that investment.

For the price of a luxury car, I gained:

- The wealth of **understanding** that comes only from direct experience
- The wealth of **empathy** that transforms abstract issues into human connections
- The wealth of **gratitude** that finds abundance in previously overlooked moments
- The wealth of **perspective** that distinguishes between what truly matters and what merely impresses
- The wealth of **authenticity** that comes from engaging with life directly rather than from behind glass

None of these forms of wealth will appear on a bank statement or tax return. They won't increase my credit score or boost my retirement account. Yet they have made me immeasurably richer in ways that matter far more profoundly.

I've come to believe that the truly wealthy person isn't the one who has the most but the one who needs the least—not because of deprivation or asceticism, but because they have discovered the riches available in experiences, connections, and moments of genuine presence.

The truly wealthy person isn't the one with the most elaborate possessions but the one with the most meaningful stories of connections formed, perspectives shifted, moments fully lived rather than merely observed.

The truly wealthy person isn't the one most effectively insulated from life's discomforts but the one most deeply engaged with life's full spectrum of experiences, the bitter and the sweet, the challenging and the joyful, the mundane and the extraordinary.

By these measures, I return from my journey far richer than when I departed, carrying wealth that cannot be stolen, devalued, or depleted—wealth that only grows when shared with others.

The loss I accepted on my Mercedes has yielded returns beyond calculation—not just in memories or stories, but in a fundamentally altered relationship with the world and my place within it. I sold a depreciating asset and gained appreciating wisdom. I surrendered a status symbol and received genuine connection. I abandoned comfort and discovered vitality.

This, I now understand, is what it truly means to get rich—not by accumulating more, but by experiencing deeply; not by protecting ourselves from life, but by participating fully in it; not by focusing on what we can possess, but by recognizing all that we can become when we step beyond the boundaries of our controlled environments into the magnificent uncertainty of the wider world.

I sold my Mercedes at a loss and got rich beyond measure. And that has made all the difference.

Conclusion

Six months ago, I sold my Mercedes at a financial loss and stepped out of my corporate bubble into the real world—choosing public transportation, street food, and direct human connection over the insulation of luxury. What began as an experiment to broaden my perspective transformed into a profound journey of personal awakening.

Traveling across India's diverse cities—from Mumbai's monsoon-drenched streets to Delhi's frost-covered mornings, from Chennai's sweltering heat to Bangalore's gentle climate—I discovered a wealth that no balance sheet could capture. The conventional markers of success I had accumulated over decades— the executive position, the investments, the material comforts spalled in comparison to the riches I found in unexpected places.

I found wealth in human connections that transcended social barriers—conversations with vegetable vendors whose philosophical insights rivaled any corporate strategist, chai sellers whose customer service outshone five-star hotels, and rickshaw pullers whose dignity and determination humbled me.

I discovered wealth in new perspectives that expanded my understanding, seeing how resilience transforms obstacles into opportunities, how kindness creates warmth in the coldest circumstances, how mental discipline transcends physical discomfort, and how finding one's authentic rhythm can lead to sustainable growth.

I gained wealth in experiences that money cannot buy—the solidarity of strangers huddling together during Mumbai's downpours, the shared warmth of a roadside bonfire on a Delhi winter night, the collective endurance of Chennai's midday heat, the creative energy of Bangalore's outdoor gatherings.

Most significantly, I acquired wealth in self-knowledge—recognizing my own patterns, privileges, and possibilities in ways that would have remained invisible had I stayed within my comfortable bubble. Each city acted as a mirror, reflecting different aspects of my character and challenging different assumptions I had carried unexamined.

I learned that:

- True resilience isn't about enduring hardship but transforming it
- Genuine kindness requires no recognition and expects no return
- Real endurance comes from mental discipline, not just physical stamina
- Authentic progress sometimes requires pausing rather than pushing
- Every journey outward is also a journey inward

As I return to the world I left behind, I do so as a different person with eyes more open, a heart more accessible, and priorities fundamentally realigned. The questions I now face aren't about what I'll purchase or possess but about how I'll integrate these lessons into my daily life and decisions.

Will I maintain the perspective shift that occurred when I stepped out of my Mercedes? Will I continue to value experiences over possessions, connections over comfort, understanding over insulation? Will I remember that true wealth cannot be parked in a garage but must be lived every day through conscious choices and genuine engagement?

The financial loss I accepted on my car has yielded returns beyond calculation—not just in memories or stories, but in a transformed relationship with the world. I sold a depreciating asset and gained appreciating wisdom. I surrendered a status symbol and received genuine connection. I abandoned comfort and discovered vitality.

This journey has taught me that the richest person isn't the one who has the most but the one who needs the least—not from deprivation, but from discovering the abundance available in moments of genuine presence and connection. The richest person isn't the one with the most elaborate possessions but the one with the most meaningful stories. The richest person isn't the one most effectively insulated from life's discomforts but the one most deeply engaged with life's full spectrum of experiences.

By selling my Mercedes at a loss, I gained riches beyond measure. By stepping out of my aquarium, I discovered the vast, unpredictable, magnificent sea of real life. And in that sea—with all its storms and calm waters, its depths and shallows, its darkness and light—I found a wealth that will sustain me long after material possessions have faded away: the wealth of a life fully lived.